EMPOWERED POSSIBILITIES:
Living Your Best Life at Any Age

BY DALE LIND

COPYRIGHT © 2012 DALE LIND
ALL RIGHTS RESERVED

ISBN-10: 0615536026
ISBN-13: 9780615536026

LIBRARY OF CONGRESS
CONTROL NUMBER: 2011938133

WATERMAN COMMUNITIES, INC., IN COLLABORATION WITH WATERMAN COMMUNITIES FOUNDATION, INC., MOUNT DORA, FL

Special Thanks to

Christine Kamuda

Holly Lamie

Jeff Lind

Jodie McEwen

Lynn Haynes

and to

Billy and Linda Morse

with

Alison Brown

for Excellent Editing

Aunt Evonne-
Thanks for being in or near some of my most treasured memories and for your very special gift of making all near you feel loved.

Riley-
Thanks for being my granddaughter. You are wise beyond your years and when I need the warmth of a smile, all I have to do is think of you.

Reed-
Thanks for being my grandson. Your energy, enthusiasm and wit bring me so much joy.

TABLE OF CONTENTS

Prologue: The Promise 1

Ch. 1: Your Life, Your Choices 5

Ch. 2: Empower Your Possibilities, An Introduction 13

Ch. 3: Occupational Wellness: Engage in Activities
That Have Meaning for You 27

Ch. 4: Self-Worth Wellness: Matter and Make a Difference . . 45

Ch. 5: Physical Wellness: Preserve Your Physical Fitness 71

Ch. 6: Emotional Wellness: Optimize Your Opportunities
with Attitudes of Resilience and Possibility 97

Ch. 7: Spiritual Wellness: Worship and Wield
the Energy That Comes from Putting
Your Faith in a Higher Power 121

Ch. 8: Intellectual Wellness: Expand Your Brainpower
through Lifelong Learning 135

Ch. 9: Social Wellness: Build and Maintain
Positive Relationships 151

Ch. 10: A Brief Summary 175

Epilogue: The Challenge 191

PROLOGUE: THE PROMISE

Naturally, I want you to read this book all the way through from beginning to end. I did, after all, spend ten years collecting the data and four very intense months writing the manuscript. I wouldn't want to think I wasted my time.

But as much as it would please me, that is not enough reason for you to read. So, let me make you a promise. Here it is and it's a good one:

I promise you that if you read this book, accept its premises and apply its principles, you will reap the following rewards:

1. You will enjoy significantly greater physical health and well-being.

2. You will notice a measurable increase in your mental acuity. You'll be sharper and more discerning, and you'll make better decisions.

Because of your improved health, fitness, and sharpened intellect, you will want, in your own unique way, to:

- Engage, participate, and get involved. If you aren't one already, it is unlikely you will become a social butterfly, but you will no longer be satisfied to merely sit back and spectate. You will play a role in *making things happen* rather than simply *wondering what happened*.

EMPOWERED POSSIBILITIES

- Matter to and make a difference in the lives of those around you. You will enjoy a stronger sense of usefulness and being needed. In the process, you will create a legacy of positive contributions and treasured memories that will achieve a value far beyond the common measures of dollars and cents.

- Preserve and promote physical fitness in your life first, then in the lives of those you care about. You will be stronger and more energetic. From time to time you may get sick, but not as often or for as long as you may now be experiencing.

- Optimize the opportunities that come your way through a heightened sense of optimism and positive thinking. In so doing, you will add both quantity and quality to your years.

- Worship, pray and/or meditate more, and center your faith in a higher power, which you may already know as God, or Spirit, etc. In the process you will see your health improve and your sense of peace, safety, and security increase.

- Expand your intellectual capacity and strengthen your brain. Not only will you learn and try new things, but also will actually want to and enjoy doing so.

- Relate to those you care about in more loving and less contentious ways. Furthermore, even at an age when you may be experiencing the loss of friends and family, you will discover new ways to make new friends.

It sounds like a lot to come from one short book, and in fact it is. I wouldn't blame you if at this point you have some doubts. All I can offer you right now, in these opening words, is this: I have

EMPOWERED POSSIBILITIES

tried everything I recommend and it all works for me. I'm pretty average, so if these principles work for me, I see no reason why they won't also work for you.

But don't just take my word for it. In a study involving 169 people over the age of one hundred, the following life patterns were found in the vast majority of them:

1. Optimistic attitudes with very little evidence of depression
2. A powerful ability to handle stress and loss
3. Regular and challenging intellectual stimulation
4. The use of humor as a coping mechanism
5. A strong network of social interaction and support
6. Very few examples of obesity, excess use of alcohol, and/or smoking

Joe (above) shares a quiet moment with a new friend

As you read this book, you will find further illustrations of each of these examples and a few more besides. It's all been done before. Why can't you do it too? Others are living successfully and in good health to great ages. Why not you?

There is an old cliché that goes like this: "You can't teach old dog new tricks."

Right now you might be thinking, "I'm an old dog and it is too late for me to change." Before you give up, consider this story of a very old dog that did learn and is still learning, as of this writing, many new tricks against all expert knowledge, opinion, and judgment. This, by the way, really is a story about a genuine old dog.

EMPOWERED POSSIBILITIES

My good friends Kevin and Jodie love dogs. Well, to be completely fair, Jodie loves dogs; Kevin loves Jodie, so Kevin tolerates dogs, often five or six at a time sharing his home and eating his food.

Recently, in order to save him from euthanasia, Jodie adopted an old dog named Joe. The experts told Jodie to just keep him comfortable until he died. He was too old, blind, deaf, crippled, and suffering from an advanced heart murmur to ever be of much use.

Not only does Jodie love dogs, but she often doesn't take direction well!! She brought Joe home, introduced him to his fellow canine housemates (and a resigned Kevin), and showed him around the house. Guiding him with a leash, she walked him from room to room and he loved it! She taught him the meaning of the word cookie using hand signals.

Today, Joe is something of a local celebrity, accompanying Jodie on public presentations promoting the advantages of adopting senior dogs. When he's not on the speaking circuit, Old Joe races around the house, easily keeping up with the younger dogs, and he routinely runs circles around Kevin. Stairs present only minor obstacles and he can beg for food from the table with the best of them.

Yes, Joe was and is an old dog, in dog years much older than most of you reading about him. Yet love, patience, determination, and gentle training taught him new tricks. He is living his best life and loving it. You too can do what Old Joe has done. You may be an old dog, but you can learn new tricks.

I promise.

CHAPTER 1:
YOUR LIFE, YOUR CHOICES

The journey of our life, in the quiet privacy of our thoughts, when we can be fully honest with ourselves, is really an endless string of results stemming from the choices we have made. Some of you will read the foregoing statement and struggle with it. We live, after all, in a blame-seeking world where rather than accept responsibility for the bad things that happen to us, our first inclination is to find someone or something we can blame.

> *All life is a journey. Which paths we take, what we look back on, and what we look forward to is up to us. We determine our destination, what kind of road we take, and how happy we are when we get there.*
>
> *– Anonymous*

Maybe it's bad weather slowing down the traffic that made me late. A favorite one that I heard often from my children when they got up late was, "My alarm didn't go off this morning."

One of the most popular of current excuses, thanks to modern psychology, is, "my parents didn't raise me right," or some variation thereof.

But when it comes right down to it, even if all of those things are true, they don't have to determine the path our lives take. We can't always control circumstances, but we can almost always control our reaction to them. In other words, in any situation no

EMPOWERED POSSIBILITIES

matter how challenging, bad, or difficult it might be, we can choose the way we respond to it.

So too, in the matter of aging successfully and living our best life, when confronted with the natural challenges that come in the aging process, we can make choices as to how we respond and what we do. To reinforce that concept, I'd like to suggest a few things for you to think about, where your choices can make all the difference in the quality of your life.

First, you can't stop aging but you can impact how you age. We live in a youth-hungry society. Our television sets bombard us with a constant barrage of advertisements offering products and services guaranteed to keep us young, or at least looking that way. Most of these products involve either taking vitamins or rubbing various creams and ointments on our body parts to smooth out the wrinkles.

Plastic surgery to alter our appearance, take away our wrinkles, and give us bigger lips and higher cheekbones is so prevalent that whenever we see an older person who looks young our first thought is, "I wonder how much work he's/she's had done? What did that face cost him/her?"

Unfortunately, most of these people are living proof that just changing your appearance doesn't extend your youth and vitality. It takes much more than smooth skin, a perky chin and supple, kissable lips to feel good.

This book is about changing your lifestyle in ways that will make you feel and act young even if you never have plastic surgery to take away the wrinkles. It is, I think, much better to feel and act young than to simply look young. It's true-the years will keep adding up, and short of death there is absolutely no way, not now nor will there ever be, to stop that. There is a way, however, to age successfully by improving the quality of your life and thereby in all probability adding to its quantity in the process.

> *People who say that life is not worthwhile are really saying that they have no personal goals which are worthwhile. Get yourself a goal worth working for. Better yet, get yourself a project. Always have something ahead of you to look forward to work for and hope for.*
>
> *– Maxwell Maltz*

Here comes the second thing I want you to think about. You're never too old to be young. But before you come down on me with the facts of life, let me hasten to clarify. Accepting that statement as true requires you also to accept the fact that age can be a state of mind. So maybe the statement would be better rendered as, "you're never too old to act and feel young." The bottom line is that the first step in acting and feeling young even as you age, is to act and feel young. Now isn't that profound?

Along with the statement above is a companion statement. Just as you are never too old to be young, it is also true that you are never too young to be old. I'm sure you won't have to think very hard to identify some people who are young in years but already quite old in their actions and attitudes. These are the people whose first waking thought is a quick inventory of their various body parts in search of a point of pain and/or illness. These are the people who are negative about almost everything. These are the people who at age thirty say "I just can't do what I used to do." Fortunately this is a treatable condition, and this book will show you how to treat it.

The next point for you to consider is this. You will never again be younger than you are today. Wow! The profound thoughts just keep flowing!! Therefore, the best time to begin aging successfully and living your best life is right now. Even though as I write these lines I'm in a hotel room alone, I can hear your objections to this last statement. They probably sound something like this:

"This guy has no idea whatsoever what it's like to be old!"

Well, I'm certainly not as old as I expect to get nor as young as I wish I was, and I definitely aged faster than I ever thought I would. I am, as I write, sixty-three years old. I could draw Social Security if I wanted to, and in less than two years I'll qualify for Medicare, but I don't think of myself as old, and I don't limit my activities to what I think a sixty-three-year-old ought to limit himself to.

In fact, just six weeks ago I decided to do something I've wanted to do for well over forty years. I joined a martial arts class. Twice a week, on Monday and Wednesday nights, I can be found in the Victory Martial Arts Gym in Apopka, Florida, working out with twenty other guys and gals, all of whom are at least ten years younger than me. Some of them, in fact, are teenagers. And guess what? While I am the oldest, I'm not the slowest. As we finish our intense warm-up exercises and start stretching, I listen very carefully to those around me and am pleased to say, I am not the only one panting. In fact, I'm not even panting the loudest or the hardest or for that matter, the longest. Now, that's something to be proud of.

> **Don't look forward to the day you stop suffering. Because when it comes, you will know you are dead.**
>
> **– Tennessee Williams**

Other thoughts you're thinking probably include, "But I am old and my back has been bad for forty-five years."

Certainly your age and your bad back have to be considered. But they don't have to prevent you from moving forward with the principles you will find in this book.

EMPOWERED POSSIBILITIES

The list of excuses you are probably thinking of could go on ad infinitum, but I think the two I've listed help to make my point. Today, you are the youngest you will ever be. I challenge you, therefore, to read on. You can live your best life and age successfully, and you can begin at any age and in almost any physical condition. The most finite resource you have is time. Consequently, determine to live your personal best life in every precious and irreplaceable moment. You can't replace the time you have already lost, but you can increase the time you have ahead of you.

Possibly by now you are hovering on the brink of conviction that maybe, just maybe, you of all people can age a little more successfully than you currently are. Move forward with that thought, but please keep in mind: there is little value in extending the quantity of your years if you don't also improve the quality of your life.

I am, at this point in my life, in the early stages of my thirty-sixth year of working in the field of aging and senior services. As a beginner all those years ago, one of the first opinions I formed was that thanks to modern medicine, we knew how to extend the number of years of a life but hadn't done much to improve the quality of that life.

I propose, in this book to share with you seven things I've learned that, based on the choices you make with the information I'll share and the challenges I'll present, will help you not only live longer but also live better. Now, where can you get a better deal than that?

The choice, in the simplest terms I can muster, is this. You can follow the principles outlined in this book and choose to live long and die short, or you can ignore them and go on much as you have and in effect be choosing to live short and die long.

EMPOWERED POSSIBILITIES

If just now, you are scratching your head wondering what I said and what it might mean to you, let me clarify. People who age successfully and live their best life, powered by good health and the will and stamina to take advantage of life's opportunities, tend to live long and healthy lives; but in the end, they too must die. The good news is that when these empowered, best-life living people come to the end of their personal road, death is almost always quick and often painless. If you have to die, and ultimately you do, staying healthy and active to the very end is as good a way to go as you can get.

> *Analyze the impact of your age by answering the following questions:*
>
> *1. How old are you?*
>
> *2. How old do you act?*
>
> *3. How old do you make those around you feel?*
>
> *4. What changes do you feel you need to make in your lifestyle?*

I regularly hear, and I'm sure you do too, the words, "If you have your health, you have everything."

As you read this book, be aware that when we speak of good health, we are including mental health along with physical health. Though usually dealt with as separate topics, I find them to be inseparable. In order to be healthy, both physically and mentally, you need to apply in your life as many of the seven principles I'll share as you reasonably can.

I hope you'll stop reading just now and answer the questions contained in the table above. These answers will help you get ready for the information and challenges soon to come in this book.

Before we move on, let's address two legitimate issues that some of you might already be preparing to challenge me with. I have promised to show you how you can increase in physical strength

EMPOWERED POSSIBILITIES

and mental sharpness. I have indicated that you can enjoy these improvements at any age. Yet even I, optimist that I am, cannot ignore two absolute truths about the aging process.

First, loss of muscle mass, beginning at about the age of 40, is a natural part of the aging process. Yes, I did just say it is a natural part of the aging process, and it is important that you know that. However, what I haven't yet said is even more important. While loss of muscle mass is a natural part of the aging process, it is not an essential part. In other words, as natural as getting weaker might be as you age, it does not have to happen. You can combat and effectively reverse it with exercise.

Let me give you just one example from my personal experience. Three years ago at the age of sixty, I began an exercise routine that included the use of several weightlifting machines. My first day on one machine in particular found me struggling to complete eight repetitions at fifty pounds. Just last week, three years later, I easily completed twelve repetitions on that same machine at ninety pounds. I nearly doubled my lifting strength capacity. If I can do it, so can you.

Second, science has long believed and taught that a natural part of the aging process is deterioration in mental sharpness. In fact, it does appear that between the ages of forty-five and eighty-five our brain can lose up to 20 percent of its weight and thirty thousand to fifty thousand neurons per day. Don't be too concerned about the high count of neuron loss; you have so many of them that a loss of fifty-thousand won't even be noticed; but sitting here it occurs to me that, given my lifelong struggle with weight, it would be nice if the brain actually weighed more. If it did, wouldn't that make weight loss also a natural part of the aging process?

Recent scientific observation suggests that as many as two out of three people will experience varying levels of mental decline

EMPOWERED POSSIBILITIES

as they age. More and more however, scientists are concluding that the one third who don't lose it mentally suggest there are reasons other than the natural progression of age for these losses. It's becoming more and more evident that a significant amount of loss of mental acuity, historically attributed to the aging process, might in fact be more the result of poor brain exercise habits. In other words, just as unused muscles will go soft, so too will unused brains.

When I was twenty-three years old, I used to amaze myself and others with my ability to keep a running total of the purchases in my shopping cart, which often proved accurate within pennies when I got to the checkout counter. I was sharp when it came to numbers.

At thirty-three, it was no longer easy. By the time I reached forty-three, it was difficult; at fifty-three, highly challenging; and today at sixty-three, virtually impossible. Was what I have just described a natural deterioration of mental ability connected to the aging process, or might there be another explanation?

Please note that my ability to use this talent for numbers was already in decline in my early thirties, and there is no evidence suggesting that natural mental decline begins that early. Something important did happen in my life between the ages of twenty-three and thirty-three that brought about this loss of numerical dexterity, and it had nothing to do with advancing years. Electronic adding machines entered my life. With the disappearance of the need to manually add long columns of numbers came the weakening and eventual loss of my ready ability to do so. The loss clearly was not the result of aging; it happened because I stopped exercising that particular talent.

You don't have to get physically weaker and mentally slower simply because you're getting older. So, let's move forward.

CHAPTER 2:
EMPOWER YOUR POSSIBILITIES, AN INTRODUCTION

At its very roots, the word "empower" means simply to give power to or to make someone or something powerful. We could stop right here in our efforts to define the word "empower," and still have a very meaningful word on which to base this book. However, to empower means not only to give power to, but to do it in a way that inspires, emboldens, and encourages. It includes energizing and galvanizing for action. In the simplest terms possible, to empower the possibilities in your life means to pep yourself up and get going. So let's go ahead and do just that.

> **To Empower**
> 1. *Give authority to somebody: to give somebody power*
> 2. *Make more confident or assertive: to give somebody a greater sense of confidence or self-esteem*

This book is about how to empower your ability to live your personal best life at any age. Included in the concept must also be a discussion on how to age successfully. Now that's a concept you are probably not familiar with. We seldom think of the aging process in terms of success. Yet by the time you finish this book I firmly believe that you will understand the importance of being successful in the aging process. After all, success in aging is ultimately defined by how well you feel, how involved you are, and how much fun you are having as an older person.

EMPOWERED POSSIBILITIES

Since successful aging has already been announced as a topic of importance, let's start there. Just what does it mean to you personally to age successfully? The answer to that question, as simple as it sounds, is really quite complex and highly personalized to the individual. You see, no two individuals are likely to define the success of their lives in the same terms.

There are however, several what we might call successful aging goals that tend to be shared by most people. These goals include such things as good health, financial security, safety, the power to make choices, the ability to be independent, great relationships, and the strength and energy to do things that we enjoy doing.

So take a moment, even though it's early in your reading process, and stop reading, just for a little while. Take some time to consider your own personal success goals for your aging process. Feel free to enter your thoughts in the table provided above.

When I am old, I will feel that I have aged successfully if the following things are true in my life:

1. _____
2. _____
3. _____
4. _____
5. _____
6. _____
7. _____

Now that you've identified some of your basic aging success goals, it's time to challenge some of the common beliefs that have been circulating about aging for far too long.

EMPOWERED POSSIBILITIES

First, age is far less a number than it is a state of mind. For as long as I can remember, society prepared me to accept the magic age of sixty-five as being old. How did that happen? What made sixty-five old? At age sixty-three as I write this book, I'm not far from that milestone, and somehow I don't feel anywhere near old. What's the deal?

As you might suspect, an actuary was involved. In 1935, thanks to the determined commitment of President Franklin D. Roosevelt, Congress created the Social Security system. Needing a number to set a goal for retirement, they chose the age of sixty-five.

At that time, carefully researched, documented, and prepared life expectancy tables show that the average American could only expect to live to about the age of fifty. On the surface, therefore, age sixty-five made good economic sense; since the life expectancy tables suggested that most people would not even live long enough to collect.

Unfortunately even then, and with growing negative impact through the years, there was a flaw in the calculations of the life expectancy tables. In the first two decades of the twentieth century, infants died at an alarming rate. As is common in this country, adversity breeds invention and by the 1920s, vast improvements took place in the medical treatment of babies. Babies didn't die as often and life expectancy increased significantly. These improvements, however, were not reflected in the tables available in 1935.

In reality, the fact was that 54 percent of all people born in the first two decades of the twentieth century who overcame the high odds of infant mortality to reach the age of twenty-one would draw Social Security and furthermore, keep drawing it for approximately thirteen more years. It seems the actuary should have been more careful. Even then, sixty-five wasn't as old as they thought it was.

EMPOWERED POSSIBILITIES

Americans weren't the first to choose sixty-five as a cost-effective retirement age. As far back as 1889, Chancellor Otto von Bismarck of Germany identified age sixty-five as the starting point for his country's retirement system. Just as was thought to be true in 1935 for the Americans, Germany, with an expected average life span of forty-five years in 1889, was not likely to experience overwhelming costs.

Simply put—and I take great comfort in this truth—if age sixty-five ever was old, it certainly isn't now. For the past several decades, life expectancy has been marching steadily towards eighty. There are far too many examples of individuals who continue to live active, productive lives well beyond the age of sixty-five for it to still be considered old. Let's look at a few of them.

Ronald Reagan comes easily to mind. When he took the office of president of the United States for the very first time, he was just one month short of his seventieth birthday. He served two full terms with energy and distinction and left the office a few weeks before his seventieth birthday.

In 2008, Senator John McCain of Arizona ran for president at the age of seventy-two. What I find even more interesting however, is that with him on the campaign trail at almost every stop, was his ninety-five-year-old mother.

Former Governor Jerry Brown of California, after a nearly thirty-year absence from office, ran again in 2010 and got reelected at the age of seventy-two. He believes he can make a difference in the horrendous mess that is California's economy. He is definitely not thinking like an old, worn down, and used up person.

Longtime action star Clint Eastwood, at age eighty, is still acting, directing, and occasionally getting the girl.

EMPOWERED POSSIBILITIES

Colonel Sanders, founder of the world-famous Kentucky Fried Chicken franchise, started his business at the age of sixty-seven.

The artist, Grandma Moses, who didn't touch a paintbrush until she was seventy-two, went on to gain worldwide recognition for her skill and creativity at the easel.

And it isn't just the famous that age so successfully. I recently met a man; I think his name was Art, hiking in the mountains above Palm Springs, California, at the age of eighty. The much younger couple with him good-naturedly complained about how hard it was to keep up with him.

The grandfather of one of the guys I work out with at Gold's Gym had to give up downhill skiing after a triple bypass at the age of eighty-five. He took up snowboarding, and at ninety-one is still doing it. Who knew that snowboarding could be so much better for an old person with a history of heart problems than downhill skiing? Each year, as recently as the winter of 2010, he leads an expedition of family members on a snowboarding excursion to the Alps.

The fact is, very little of what we know about growing old has to be true. For example, it's a well-proven fact that older people can increase muscle strength throughout the whole course of their lives. Up until about the age of eighty, older people can actually build new muscle fibers through exercise. Beyond the age of eighty, building new muscle fibers is not likely, but the existing ones can be strengthened and made to grow.

Further, older people can continue to expand their brainpower. The process for doing this is really rather simple. Never stop learning. Never stop experimenting. Never stop going new places and trying new things. Nurture your spirit of experimentation and adventure and it will nurture you.

EMPOWERED POSSIBILITIES

Injuries due to falls and elevated frequency of illness are almost synonymous with aging. Yet older people can reduce their risks of falling as well as getting sick. Through the right kind of exercise they can improve their balance, and with a combination of exercise and nutrition they can strengthen their immune systems.

In fact, according to a study on aging done by the MacArthur Foundation, 70 percent of the impact of the aging process is determined by the lifestyle choices we make every day. Imagine that!! 70 percent of the way we age is determined by our own choices and decisions.

I could go on but I think you get the point. As I said earlier, aging really is more a state of mind than it is a number. As long as you live, you'll add to the number of years in your life. But as the number grows, so can your satisfaction and enjoyment if you live those years right.

So what is there about some of these old people that allows them to keep on going and going and going, never seeming to wear down? Are you sure, Mr. Author, that the secret isn't just a simple matter of being born into the right family with good heredity?

I used to think so until I did a survey of the seniors I work with, most of who were at least eighty-five years old at the time, and discovered that very few claimed to come from a family line of people who lived long healthy lives. I naturally concluded there had to be other reasons and have spent the last ten years identifying them. The inheritance of good genes certainly helps. Coming from a family line generously sprinkled with ancestors who lived long, happy, healthy, and productive lives is a definite advantage, but it is far from the only way to age successfully and live your best life.

When I first began this journey, I focused on discovering what makes active and productive older people tick. As I got further

EMPOWERED POSSIBILITIES

into it however, I realized that the life principles I was discovering, if lived properly and faithfully, will determine success at any age. In fact, the earlier in life you begin applying these principles, the more success you will enjoy. So if you're a young person, keep reading. Even though I've based this book on what I've learned in thirty-five years' experience working in senior services, you can learn from it, grow with it, and empower the possibilities in your life at any age.

I'm anxious to just dive right in and start introducing you to the seven exciting and life-changing principles for aging successfully while living your personal best life. More than anything else right now, I would love to empower you for independence.

> *Age is a quality of mind; if you've left your dreams behind, if hope is cold, if you no longer look ahead, if your ambitious fires are dead, then you are old!*
>
> *– Anonymous*

I long to guide you through the door of empowered possibilities, but before I can, there is one final misguided belief about aging that must be challenged. It is a belief that at first glance seems sensible but after careful study turns out to be dangerous and damaging to the future of people as they age. That dangerous and damaging belief that we must now confront is "old people have to be taken care of."

Many do and I can't and won't deny that. In fact, if it weren't true, I'd be doing something else to make a living and certainly wouldn't be writing this book. A few paragraphs ago I cited statistics showing that 70 percent of the impact of aging results from our choices. That leaves just 30 percent beyond our control.

We can't stop the natural progression of wrinkles, but we don't have to choose to make them worse by smoking. Some disease processes are hereditary. There's not much we can do about that. Left to their own devices, the body and the mind will both

EMPOWERED POSSIBILITIES

weaken with age, but neither will if we keep exercising them. If, while crossing a street with all lights in my favor, a careless, preoccupied, and self-centered driver distractedly babbling on a cell phone runs a red light, hits and kills me, that qualifies as an event beyond my control. But when we can exercise control, we should. Many of the things we struggle with as we age are the results of choices made earlier in our lives. The good news is that many if not most of our choice-based problems can be improved through a series of different and better choices. Our bodies and minds possess remarkable capacity to heal.

For example, I love food. Consequently I have consistently chosen to overindulge, resulting in extra weight. I can choose to change my eating habits. Positive results will take longer to accrue than they would have thirty, twenty, even ten years ago, but they will happen.

I'm often inconsistent in my exercise habits. As a result, my stamina isn't what it should and could be. Some would say that the stamina drain is a natural process of aging, but it isn't. I can choose more consistent exercise and improve my stamina.

In fact, there are many declines usually associated with aging that can be reversed once we choose to exercise control. Here are some examples:

Older people often find themselves sidelined and ignored as life goes on about them. Though in possession of a wealth of experience-based knowledge, seldom is their opinion sought. What happened? They retired, that's what. Probably in the beginning they thought it would be good to have no responsibilities, but now they find it boring. Just as they chose to retire and drop out, they can choose to engage, get involved, stop being a spectator and become a participant, and once again enjoy respect and recognition.

EMPOWERED POSSIBILITIES

1. Older people sometimes complain that their lives just don't matter anymore; that they are too old, too sick, and too tired to be of use to anybody. If this is your current situation, let me assure you, it doesn't have to continue. You have much to give and more than likely, time needed to devote to giving it. You can make a difference, but you may have to be the one to reach out.

2. The stereotypical image of an older person is one with severely reduced physical capabilities. If you are old and lack the strength to do the things you enjoy, it is likely because you chose to stop exercising. The very good news is that at any age, if you choose to exercise your strength will increase. If you are now paying the price for poor eating habits, make better dining choices and your health will improve no matter how old you are. The human body enjoys remarkable capacity to heal itself when treated properly.

3. The biggest impact you can make on the quality of your life is through changing your attitude. Usually, what we think about comes true. If we think about our limitations, our limitations grow. Therefore, it's only reasonable to conclude that if we think about our possibilities, they too will materialize and grow.

4. Another important choice we can make is to put our faith in a higher power. There is great comfort in knowing you are not alone when faced with challenge. There is tremendous freedom in ready access to celestial strength and wisdom. We can choose to be a person of faith, or we can choose to go it alone. Choose faith.

EMPOWERED POSSIBILITIES

5. Older people are commonly believed to suffer reduced mental capacity. In fact, if this is happening to you, the odds are two out of three that it is because you chose to disengage your brain and let it go to sleep. Choosing to expand your learning will strengthen your mental capacity.

6. Loneliness and boredom are commonly recognized problems for older people. Death is inescapable no matter how well you care for yourself. It is impossible to age and not lose relationships. If you find yourself with no friends, even if the ones you had have all died, only your choice will prevent you from making new ones.

You do not have to be sidelined just because you are old. You can matter and make a difference at any age. You can improve your strength and health. You can even choose the attitude with which you respond to life's challenges. You can increase your independence. It is never too late to get in touch with your spiritual side, expand the horizons of your mind, and form new relationships, but you do have to make the choices that lead you in those directions.

What old people really need is not to be taken care of. What old people really need is empowered, maximum independence allowing them to exercise the choices that will assure that they can age successfully and live their best lives. Empowered independence expands the possibilities for living your best life successfully at any age.

Don't expect to hear too much in this book, beyond what already has been said, on the subject of heredity—largely because I don't know much about it, and since I can't control it have little interest in studying it. I will say just this: it is very difficult to age in good health to one hundred without heredity on your side. There is every reason to believe however, that the healthy nine-

EMPOWERED POSSIBILITIES

ties are achievable even without good heredity on your side, if you make good choices. And given the recent, rapid advances in our understanding of the aging process, I wouldn't rule out one hundred.

In this book I will share with you seven life-changing secrets extracted from the lives of older people who continue to live well and productively into their eighties, nineties and even hundreds. The word "empower," as I use it in this book, is an acronym representing the seven secrets that I hope will become, for you, foundational life principles.

The Empowerment Model, as presented here, is based on seven fundamental principles of whole-person wellness. Perhaps you are more used to a wellness model with four or five elements, but as I considered the impact of aging and what is needed to empower independence in older people, I concluded that seven elements of wellness were more appropriate. The seven elements of whole-person wellness as I have defined them are:

- **Occupational Wellness:** To be wholly well, it is necessary to occupy your time with meaningful activity.

- **Self-Worth Wellness:** The ability to contribute, give back, make a difference, and be needed can be—depending on the intensity of your needs—more important than having your needs met.

- **Physical Wellness:** The body must be kept in prime condition.

- **Emotional Wellness:** A positive attitude with a focus on life's possibilities significantly increases the quantity and especially the quality of life.

EMPOWERED POSSIBILITIES

- **Spiritual Wellness:** Wellness improves when there is reliance on and faith in a higher power outside the self.

- **Intellectual Wellness:** To be wholly well involves expanding and preserving mental acuity.

- **Social Wellness:** Relationships and a broad range of networks are essential to life success and whole-person wellness.

The principles for Empowered Independence as briefly described below are based on the seven principles of whole-person wellness just listed.

Occupational Wellness: The first **E** in empower stands for engagement. People who truly want to empower possibilities in their lives are not satisfied to simply be spectators cheering and occasionally jeering from the sidelines. They want to be part of the action. They are focused on being part of the solution. They are engaged. They participate. They get involved and leave their mark. And possibly most importantly, their engagement is primarily on things they care about, enjoy, and are naturally talented for.

Self-Worth Wellness: The **M** in empower stands for matter and make a difference. It's about the importance of leaving a legacy you can be proud of. It involves having a mission in your life that is based on your natural talents, skills and preferences. Above all, it assures that in any stage and in any position of life you are needed.

Physical Wellness: The **P** in empower stands for preserve your physical fitness. Yes, there is no satisfactory way to succeed in life and the aging process without taking care of your body. This requires a combined and balanced approach of exercise and proper nutrition. The good news here is that it is never too late and you are never too old to benefit from exercise and eating right. It is also true that it is never too early.

Emotional Wellness: The **O** in empower represents optimizing your opportunities with a positive attitude. The many benefits of a positive attitude include better health, a longer and more satisfying life, more and better friendships, and greater success.

Spiritual Wellness: The **W** in empower introduces the topic that often is not politically correct. In spite of that however, it does represent a key concept present in the lives of those who have aged successfully. Put simply, worshiping and having faith in a higher power leads inevitably to a tremendous sense of peace that improves the quality of your life and increases its quantity.

Intellectual Wellness: The second **E** in empower highlights the importance of expanding your brainpower. Learn something new every day. Try something new; explore places you've never been before; empower your life with a sense of adventure. A pattern of lifelong learning not only assures that you are up to date and on top of things, but it could also reduce and maybe even eliminate the risks of losing mental capacity as you age.

Social Wellness: The **R** in empower emphasizes the importance of relationships. It is very difficult to succeed in business or any other part of your life without a good network of contacts. People, with very few exceptions, are social by nature. The quality of your friendships and the variety of contexts in which you make and keep them have a tremendous impact on your ability to empower your possibilities.

With this brief introduction concluded, it's time for me to share in greater detail the seven life-changing secrets of how to empower the possibilities in your life. As you do, you will also enhance and preserve that most precious of assets—personal, empowered independence.

CHAPTER 3:
OCCUPATIONAL WELLNESS:
ENGAGE IN ACTIVITIES THAT HAVE MEANING FOR YOU

To engage means to be involved and participate in life with an intensity that absorbs your time and engrosses your interest. When you are engaged in an activity that you care about, you are connected and enmeshed in a life with virtually unbreakable bonds that you find pleasant, satisfying, and even exciting to bear. You are pleased to expend effort when you care about the activity.

> **To Engage**
>
> 1. To require the use or devotion of something
> 2. To involve somebody in an activity, or become involved or take part in an activity
> 3. To hold the attention of, or win the affection of somebody
> 4. To become interlocked, or bring something together and cause something to interlock

In the context of the definition above, engagement sounds pretty good, doesn't it? Imagine spending your life doing only those things that you enjoy and care deeply about. In fact, isn't the whole purpose of retirement being able to do just that? I think it is, but it isn't just in retirement that you should be spending our time doing only those things that you enjoy and

EMPOWERED POSSIBILITIES

are good at. It should also be true for as many aspects of your life as possible, at any stage and at any age. And it should be most especially true in your choice of careers.

Here's a key point that must be made right up front: seldom does life come looking for you. Unless you are a well-established and much-in-demand celebrity of some sort, you should not expect opportunity to seek you out. More than likely, if you discover opportunities you can take advantage of, it will be because you went looking for them. So keep in mind, since you can't expect life to come looking for you, you must go looking for it.

If you are lonely, engage in making friends. If you are bored, get out of your shell and go looking for engaging activities. If you are consumed with aches, pains, and assorted flavors of discomfort, engage in something that takes your mind off of them. You'll be surprised how soon you start feeling better. And again I must remind you, age is no barrier to leading a life of engaged participation and involvement.

As you search life for the right opportunities, you must do so in full awareness of what it is you enjoy doing and are good at. No matter what stage of life you are currently in, you have every right to expect to enjoy and even excel at what you do. The first step is to know yourself: your natural strengths, talents, preferences, skills, and yes, even your weaknesses. Armed with that knowledge, you can identify and develop opportunities, then select the ones that fit you best. If you have done that, engagement will come naturally.

Sadly, I suspect that many if not most people do not ever find the career that fits them best. I say this because of two research studies I've read. The first one suggested that as many as 80 percent of all workers do not really like their jobs. The second research study showed that no more than 20 percent of all workers

> *Occupational Wellness: Engage and get involved. Don't just be spectators, watching from the sidelines as life passes you by.*

get to do the things they enjoy most and are best at in their jobs on a regular basis. Knowing this goes a long way toward explaining the poor service and shoddy work that we so often endure. If you really don't like what you are doing, you are probably not very good at it. If that is so, how can you possibly experience the sheer joy of heartfelt, truly motivating, and satisfying engagement? The good news is it's never too late to find your unique and special brand of engagement. You might have missed out during your career. You don't have to continue missing out in retirement, if you choose your activities wisely.

Along with engagement come certain rights that you may not have considered. For most people, hardly a day goes by without at least one opportunity to be upset. If you are merely a spectator in life, you really have no right to be upset. If you are engaged, however, not only do you have the right to be upset, you also have the right—even the responsibility—to do something about it. And in that lies a very special brand of power. It is much nicer to be a part of making things happen than it is to sit back waiting for things to happen.

Who can forget the challenging words uttered by President Kennedy during his inaugural address? "Ask not what your country can do for you - ask what you can do for your country."

I say to you, ask not what your universe can do for you - ask what you can do for your universe. Stop asking life to bring good things to you. Instead, *bring good things to life*. Engaging in life as a fully participating partner is really very satisfying.

Here's a warning. Obstacles are a part of life. Becoming engaged in the career or pastime you find most interesting and satisfying may not come easily. My longtime friend and sometime business associate Russ Phillips learned about career obstacles at a very early age. Like many little boys, Russ dreamed of being a fireman. As soon as he was old enough, he applied and was ac-

EMPOWERED POSSIBILITIES

cepted into the Rochester, New York, fire department. Very soon, however, a major obstacle to Russ's dreams blocked his way.

Russ doesn't hear very well. Even with both of his hearing aids in and turned to full volume, it can be challenging for him to follow a conversation, particularly in a crowd. Through no fault of his own, his poor hearing, a condition he was been born with, ended his dream of being a fireman. It didn't, however, end his passion for firefighting. It merely redirected it.

Never losing sight of his engaging passion, Russ became a draftsman. In the process, he devoured everything he could find on the subject of fire safety. Then, in 1976 at the age of twenty-five, Russ started his own fire safety consulting firm, Phillips and Associates. The associate was his faithful wife Jeannie, and his base of operations, his basement.

Today, Phillips and Associates is one of the most respected names, nationally, in fire safety consulting. Housed in his own office building near Rochester, New York, Russ employs fifteen consultants besides himself. He is fully engaged in a most satisfying and productive way. He enjoys remarkable success and respect in his field of fire safety. That's not bad for a young man who couldn't hear well enough to be a fireman.

Russ is living proof that if you can't engage your dreams in the exact way you have dreamed them, you can remold them into something you can achieve, being sure to retain the heart and soul of what matters to you. Russ may never have personally fought a fire larger than the occasional neglected steak on the grill, but thanks to his deep understanding of what causes death and damage in fires and how to minimize their impact on people and property, he has saved hundreds, possibly even thousands, of lives and millions of dollars.

If you're retired, you probably aren't looking for engagement opportunities on the scale I just described. But you can enjoy the engaging passion of a Russ Phillips on any scale you choose, even on a small scale.

Paul Artel was a resident in my first nursing home. For many years, Paul was our in-house mailman. As a mailman, he was fully and passionately engaged. He didn't just deliver the internal mail; he spread the news (though some might call it gossip), shared a joke or story, and in general made everyone feel better. You might wonder what was so special, engaging, and satisfying about being a nursing home mailman.

At age thirteen, an unfortunate encounter with a passing freight train cost him both arms from just below the shoulders. Though his life was spared, his arms were taken. Lacking family support and appropriate training, Paul lived the rest of his life as a ward of the state. Actually, for Paul, the role of nursing home mailman, storyteller, and town crier was the high point of his life. Satisfying

---

Satisfying engagement is a uniquely personal matter and it isn't limited to big achievements. Use the space below to make a brief list of activities you could get involved in that are personally meaningful to you.

1. _____

2. _____

3. _____

4. _____

5. _____

What, if any, obstacles are standing in your way?

_____

_____

What do you propose to do about these obstacles?

_____

_____

engagement is a uniquely personal matter and it isn't limited to big achievements. The only requirement, really, is that the activities you choose to engage in have personal and significant meaning to you.

Failure to engage can produce unwanted results such as depression. If ever an individual had the right to be depressed, it was Paul Artel. In the years I knew him, I cannot recall him ever being down or sad. Depression, a major factor in deteriorating satisfying engagement, is a uniquely personal matter.

The decline of health of many people, and especially older people, is often driven by a sense of uselessness. Engaging in the life that is going on around you can be the best antidote to debilitating depression.

Dr. Poffenberger, another resident from my early nursing home days, had been, in the 1930s, a psychologist of some renown. In his nineties at the time I knew him, his mind was always sharp and active even if his body did need occasional days off to rest and recuperate. On his good days, he was still a psychologist, moving from room to room visiting with, listening to, counseling, and encouraging his "patients." He remained engaged up until a few days before he died. He lived the best life he could for as long as he could and then he died. That's not a bad epitaph.

Just today, I attended a concert performed by a fairly new and up-and-coming British rock group named The Zimmers. Their musical menu ranges in style from the Beatles to Eric Clapton to 50's rock, Frank Sinatra, and even Rap.

Their broad range of well-performed music is not the only thing about them that is unique. You would expect a relatively new and increasingly popular rock group to be comprised of very young performers. That is definitely not the case with The Zimmers. Their average age is seventy-five. The youngest is over seventy, and the oldest is right at one hundred. The one-hundred-year-old, by the way, is one of the female lead vocalists, and her high-toned, clear-as-a-bell soprano moves you.

How many people do you know who can say their grandmother or grandfather is a lead singer in a world-renowned rock band? Quite possibly none of you can. What motivated a group of old, bored, and retired people to form a rock group?

About three years ago the British Broadcasting Company, better known as the BBC, launched an investigation into the plight of old people. They found, in their study, a disturbing pattern of loneliness, boredom, endless days with nothing to do, and dismal disengagement from life. Somewhere along the line they hatched the idea of sponsoring a rock group composed entirely of senior citizens.

To think was to act, and very soon a national recruitment campaign for older people who could sing took shape. Not sure what the results would be, the BBC was very pleased to discover that there was no shortage of applicants.

Today, just three short years later, the group performs all over the world to a growing audience of faithful fans and has even had one of their songs make it into the top thirty on the pop charts.

The Zimmers are a diverse group coming from a wide range of professions including physical therapist, cabdriver, construction worker, and professional actor. About the only things they have in common besides their age are their roots in the British Isles and their general lack of previous professional singing experience. Since death is the inescapable endpoint of the aging process, the Zimmers have suffered quite recently the loss of their first lead singer at the enviable age of ninety-three. They miss him, but they have moved on, and there is a new—and I might add, excellent—lead singer.

EMPOWERED POSSIBILITIES

That the Zimmers are fully engaged in aging successfully and living their best lives is one of the more obvious conclusions I've drawn this week. But don't take my word for it. Here's what several of their members had to say:

"Retirement can be the most exciting time of your life if you grasp it."

"To the governments of the world I say, ignore us at your peril."

"I think my children are pleased that I'm in this group. After all, they don't have to find a home for me just yet."

"My grandson, in a job interview, named me as the most interesting person he knows. He got the job!"

Gene, aged eighty-five and not a member of the Zimmers, left his easy-chair-centered life of retired boredom, at his wife's urging, and took a job as a bus driver in a senior community. He says he has much in common with the people he transports. They can't hear very well. Neither can he. They sometimes have trouble walking. So does he. He rather proudly announced that when he started, he was paid nine dollars per hour. He now earns twelve. He shared the following tidbits of wisdom:

"Old age doesn't have to be serious if you treat it with respect."

"Death is a reality of the aging process. If I lose a friend today, I make a new one tomorrow."

The Zimmers and Gene offer living proof of the value of engaging in life. They fully exemplify the truth that it is far more satisfying to be a participant than a spectator.

Being engaged in life is the heart and soul of our first element of wellness, **Occupational Wellness.** If you are satisfied with and

EMPOWERED POSSIBILITIES

enjoy the way you spend your time, you are well on the road to Empowered Independence.

Unfortunately, far too few older people find satisfying ways to engage in life beyond taking their medications, seeing their doctor, and just getting through the day. My father was such a person. One of my deepest regrets is that when he died in the early morning hours of St. Patrick's Day, 1987, I had little more than the faintest clue, even after twelve years in the business of serving senior citizens, about what it meant to age successfully and live your best life.

> **The Myth:** *It's the natural order of things for older people to retire, step aside, and let the young people handle things.*
>
> **The Facts:** *With age comes insight and wisdom that should be shared.*

Dad grew up poor in the nearly treeless, dirt road hill country of South Central Nebraska. He was the oldest of seven children, five boys and two girls, and when his mother died he took primary responsibility for the raising of his three youngest siblings. Home was a sod house measuring 28 feet long by 14 feet wide. At just under 400 ft.² of living space it would barely be considered an efficiency unit in most apartment buildings of today. Yet nine people called it home. As an aside, I've often wondered how, after dad came along, grandpa and grandma managed to the find time and privacy to produce the other six.

In 1928, just as the entire world teetered on the precipice of financial collapse, dad turned twenty-one. He spent the '30s overhauling automobile engines for a fee of seven dollars plus the cost of parts, and following the harvests throughout the dustbowl states made famous by novelist John Steinbeck in his classic, *The Grapes of Wrath*. Financial collapse and severe draught had little impact on the quality of dad's life. He'd been born poor and lived poor, and nothing much changed.

EMPOWERED POSSIBILITIES

Two of the larger families in the hill country were the Linds and the Callahans, and they filled a very useful purpose for each other. Three of the Linds married three of the Callahans. There was even, it has been said, a Callahan for dad had he so desired. But for some reason he didn't make that choice. He waited until nearly the age of forty to find my mother, a distant outlier from the state of Illinois, and I for one am glad he did.

As a young man, dad had two passions. His knowledge of and innate feeling for all things mechanical seemed to have approached genius level. Even I, at an age when teenagers weren't giving their parents much credit, could notice and appreciate his natural ability to sense and feel what was going on in a machine shop. A well-run shop, he said, had a distinct rhythm. I can remember on more than one occasion, engines being moved from car to car in our backyard under the big mulberry tree.

Dad's second passion was music. Saturday night dancing in the homes and maybe even the barns of friends and neighbors was the major source of entertainment in those treeless and windswept hills of his youth. And just as dad seemed naturally gifted to sense the inner workings of machinery, he had an uncanny ability to move the music that he heard through his ears into his brain, to be processed and then sent out through his fingers to the strings and bows of his violins.

With only two actual lessons to his credit, dad never learned to read a note of music. Yet, it seldom took him more than an intense few minutes to hear a song and learn to play it. When dad played, he played with his whole body. He seemed to become the music, and listeners from other rooms could tell the difference when he put bow to fiddle.

Later, as a soldier in World War II, dad picked up a third passion—cooking and baking. As much as I would like to tell you that he excelled at cooking and baking just as he had with his engines and his fiddle, I simply can't. Oh yes, he approached cooking and baking with the same intuitive creativity that made him a good mechanic and a brilliant fiddle player but with far different results. Though I saw him cook things that even he wouldn't eat, he never admitted to his dying day that he was no cook and baker.

It was as a soldier in World War II that dad met my mother through an introduction by one of her older brothers, an Army buddy. After the war they married and settled down in her home state of Illinois, and within a year I arrived on the cutting edge of that demographic phenomenon known as the baby boom. At thirty-nine years old, dad found himself with a family to support in a town that was every bit as foreign to him as had been the many European towns his Ninth Armored Division passed through on their way to the Rhine in World War II.

Thus dad, capitalizing on his mechanical acuity, began a series of factory jobs that included making razor blades, welding furnaces together, building ornamental iron railings, and assembling city sewage processing and disposal plants. In the twenty-six years that dad worked during my lifetime, I never knew him to fully like his job or his boss.

> Dad's mower spent nearly thirty years rusting companionably with old cars and worn-out farm implements.

Though he was good with machines, good enough in fact to invent a self-propelled lawnmower years before such mowers appeared on the market, he labored at mainly menial tasks. He could invent. What he couldn't do was figure out what to do with the invention. He had the creativity but lacked the focus. The lawnmower, ingenious as it was for its time, spent its life rusting in a farmyard with old cars and farm machinery. In one sense, that it spent decades in an abandoned farmyard always seemed appropriate to me. It was, after all, manufactured from odd parts of other abandoned machines, including the emergency brake handle of the old Graham Paige automobile my father used to drive. To further illustrate his creativity, I should tell you that he often said he got his inspiration for the lawnmower from his memories of tanks in World War II cutting down everything in their paths.

In the deepest recesses of his heart, my dad longed for the pre-World War II days of electrifying dancing crowds with his unique and from the-heart style of fiddle playing. In his new home in Illinois, he had his family; he had trees that he loved so much that he seldom traveled back to Nebraska without a few small ones in pots for his brothers to replant; but somehow he lost his music. For him to enjoy playing the fiddle there had to be a crowd eager to dance. A couple of other fiddles would be good and a guitar or two just to round out the sound, but nobody in his new home cared about the fiddle, much less square dancing.

Through the years, due to lack of practice, his fiddle skills largely disappeared and along with them went a big piece of his heart. Though he seldom played, he kept his passion for the fiddle alive through periodic trips to antique shops where, if a fiddle was on sale, he would buy it. I knew him to own no less than twenty violins at one time. And any time a child let it be known that he/she might be interested in the violin, my dad gave him or her one.

In his later years, I think he tried to get his music back. I have in my possession three of his most treasured violins, including his most favored of all, so treasured in fact that he gave it a name—Blackie. Several years ago I had all three restored to playing condition, though I certainly cannot play them. They sit in their cases in my

EMPOWERED POSSIBILITIES

office and one day I hope to display them. Blackie's case carries especially poignant memories for me. For in the last years of his life he carried it everywhere he went just in case he found another fiddler or guitar player he could jam with. In fact it still has the Amtrak identification tag attached to the handle, a relic from one of his visits to my home, then located in upstate New York.

Dad and Blackie bow some tunes.

Once, in New York City of all places, I did find a guitar player he could jam with, and what a time they had. Most of the time, however, the violin traveled back home with him without sounding a single note. Usually the case wasn't even opened.

In the end my dad knew what he wanted to engage in. He knew what he was passionate about. He just simply didn't know how to connect. I will always be sad about that. And that is why at least in part, my mission is to help you empower your best life— and showing you how to engage is as good a place to start as any.

Fortunately, others I have known have been more successful than was my dad in finding and pursuing their engaging passions. Bill had a lifelong but untested interest in pencil sketching. At eighty-nine years old he took it up and is really quite good at it. What is it that you have often thought you might enjoy but never made time for? Bill's experience proves that it's never too late to try.

John never sang publically until the age of eighty-three. Now he joyously sings in every production he can. And not only does he sing, but he dramatizes each song with careful and sometimes intricate choreography.

Ellie, too, did not sing publicly until an age somewhat close to that of Frank. Her husband finally convinced her to try out for a singing role and she wowed us all, not only with the quality of her voice, but with the passion of her performance. John and Ellie fully engage and have great fun doing it.

Then there is Rose. At age seventy-six while watching the TV show *Dancing with the Stars*, she decided she would learn ballroom dancing. Now, not only does she dance, but she dances competitively all around the country and wins, sometimes performing as many as fifty dances per day.

I can never forget Herb, the father of my first girlfriend. Truth be told, I've never forgotten the girlfriend either, but that's not really a story I care to tell. Herb was a man who appreciated and respected money with a fixed determination to extract every possible iota of value from each dollar.

As his kids were growing up, Herb decided they needed piano lessons. He bought a nice piano and signed them up for lessons. Unfortunately Herb learned, as so many parents do, that his children didn't share his passion for the piano. Herb was completely opposed to waste. If his children wouldn't play the piano, then by golly he would. So at the tender age of fifty-seven, Herb took piano lessons. He played for me once. He wasn't very good, and he knew it, but he really seemed to enjoy it.

Obstacles are a part of life. I came across this quote by Winston Churchill just yesterday: "The pessimist sees the difficulties in every opportunity, while the optimist sees the opportunities in every difficulty." A colleague recently shared the following story of her father. I think you'll see how it applies.

EMPOWERED POSSIBILITIES

An active, vital, and involved man into his seventies, my colleague's father had a stroke which at first seemed to deprive him of the ability to do the things he'd spent a lifetime learning and enjoying. Rather than wallow in depression, which most would agree he certainly had the right to do, he delved deep down into some almost forgotten interests and took up painting. Today at seventy-nine years old, he is a highly accomplished artist, impairments from the stroke and all. What difficulties are standing in your way?

As I have said before, it is better to be a participant than a bystander or spectator. Get involved in something you care about. It will add both quality and quantity to your life. Engagement comes with some pretty significant payoffs.

These payoffs include

- a deep sense of pride in yourself and the community and/or organization you are involved with;
- feelings of satisfied happiness;
- the excitement and stimulation of having fun;
- the power that can only come from exercising choice;
- the pleasure of doing what you like to do; and
- the sheer satisfaction that comes with knowing that you have accomplished something worth doing.

So what is stopping you? Get started now. As I briefly share with you the things we have built in to the lifestyle of our Waterman Communities, I hope it will generate some ideas.

The beautiful thing about engagement in things that you personally care about is that nobody tells you what to engage in. For some in our communities, it's involvement in the many committees organized to give input and direction to our various departments.

EMPOWERED POSSIBILITIES

Over one hundred of our residents volunteer their time with these committees and apply their experience and expertise to menu development, marketing initiatives, activities programming, spiritual life (*this committee has spearheaded the development of our fellowship hall and serves as the board for our on-campus interdenominational church*), and sports activities (*major responsibilities of this group include managing our lawn bowling club, assisting with our wellness and fitness program, and coordinating the use of our corporate golf club membership*).

One of our newest and most active committees is the resident finance committee that meets monthly with our chief financial officer, our budget director, and a representative from our Board of Directors to review and offer advice on the financial performance of our company. When all five resident members are in the room, our company benefits from advice developed through more than two hundred fifty years of combined, successful business experience.

In addition to these on-campus engagement opportunities, many of our residents maintain their close ties to their former churches and community clubs. Several volunteer as ushers at the local theater, and some offer their services for Chamber of Commerce functions. Again, the point is, the choice is theirs.

The choice is yours. I hope I've given you some ideas.

By the way, speaking of engaging in meaningful activities, I just read that Playboy in Chief, Hugh Hefner, eighty-four, recently got engaged to yet another Playboy Bunny. When asked about their sixty-year age difference, the Bunny is reported to have replied, "Actually, I feel like the parent in this relationship." Hmmm... Mama where are you?

While I don't pretend to understand all of the motivating factors in this relationship, it certainly seems to me that Mr. Hefner

EMPOWERED POSSIBILITIES

is living his personal best life in a most engaging way. I say, "Go Hef."

Before moving on to the next chapter, take a moment to study the table below. On it you will find several strategies suggested in this chapter that will help you be more engaged. Study each one to determine which you need to implement in your life. Then, in the space to the left of each strategy, enter a date by which you propose to have implemented that strategy in your life.

MY ENGAGEMENT AND INVOLVEMENT IMPROVEMENT PLAN	
DATE	**ENGAGEMENT & INVOLVEMENT IMPROVEMENT TACTICS**
	Develop a personal, written definition of a level of engagement that would be satisfying for you.
	Identify several activities where your role is primarily that of a spectator but you'd like to be more engaged and involved.
	Make a list of the obstacles that stand in the way of engagement and identify strategies for overcoming those obstacles.
	Make a list of people you'd like to know better and develop strategies for getting better acquainted.
	Get involved in the afairs of life around you. Don't just be a spectator.
	Identify activities, then get involved in ways that use your skills and interests.
	Offer input to conversations when in groups.
	Join and get involved in a religious organization.

EMPOWERED POSSIBILITIES

MY ENGAGEMENT AND INVOLVEMENT IMPROVEMENT PLAN	
DATE	ENGAGEMENT & INVOLVEMENT IMPROVEMENT TACTICS
	Become active in a civic or service organization. Start frequenting places where it is likely you can make friends.
	Take up a hobby you have considered through the years but never quite got around to.
	Get involved in your community through attendance at city council and other planning meetings.

CHAPTER 4:
SELF-WORTH WELLNESS:
MATTER AND MAKE A DIFFERENCE

At its core, self-worth wellness is about how you feel about yourself. It is fine to be well-thought-of and respected by your peers, but it is essential to your health and well-being that you be well-thought-of and respected by yourself. This does not mean that you must be perfect in everything you are or do. A healthy self-respect includes an understanding and acceptance of your flaws as well as your positive attributes. It is about holding an opinion of yourself that is balanced, honest, and open. It is the ability to look yourself in the eye honestly and say, "I'm not perfect but there are more good things about me than bad. In my own imperfect way I can and am making a positive difference in the lives of those I touch."

> *To matter*
> 1. *Be important, count*
> 2. *Be significant*
> 3. *Carry some weight*
> 4. *Make a difference*
> 5. *Have a bearing*
> 6. *Be relevant*
> 7. *Have substance*

To be fully healthy, everyone needs to know that they matter, that they have made and can still make a positive difference. At stake here is much more than simply how you feel about yourself. Your level of self-esteem—some prefer the term self-respect—is one of the most accurate predictors of your potential for health and longevity. Put simply, people with a balanced, honest, and positive opinion of themselves do better, live longer, and are better liked and much healthier.

Bear with me for a moment as I digress with a Christianity-based philosophical observation. In some ways, the traditional Christian approach to the worthlessness of the self is an obstacle to good self-esteem. Embedded deeply in the Christian tradition is the often-expressed belief that human beings, at their core, are essentially rotten and therefore incapable of doing any good thing except through Christ. I really don't want to debate Christian doctrine and I honestly don't know much about the views of other world religions on this topic, but I would like to say simply this. Christians also believe that human beings are created in the image of God and are the treasured objects of his love. Years ago I heard a pastor put it this way: "God doesn't make junk." I think, therefore, that not only does God not mind if we feel good about ourselves, but I think he expects us to. From my limited study it seems that the Gods depicted in most other major belief systems also want you to feel good about yourself. In this case, while the path may be radically different religiously speaking, the destination is the same.

> *Self-worth wellness: Matter and make a difference. Enjoy the sweet satisfaction that can only come from knowing you are loved, valued and needed.*

If therefore your God is willing to give you permission to feel good about yourself, why shouldn't you also give yourself that same permission?

From the time we're born, long before we can express our needs wants and desires in any form other than our cries, we have what seems to be a built-in need to know that we are loved, important, and valued. This need intensifies as we grow older. Ultimately it expresses itself in the things that we do. Our focus on our need to matter, contribute, and make a difference is never very far from our thoughts, even if it remains mostly in our subconscious.

I cannot recall ever meeting anyone who at some level didn't want to be valued and appreciated by others. No one that I've ever known expressed his or her life's goal as mediocrity. Imagine your response if you heard someone say in a loud and bragging tone, "Hey, I nailed mediocrity today, and I think I can pull it off again tomorrow. Why heck, in just a couple of weeks I'm on track to be average."

Most people want to be successful at something. We need to know that we are better in at least one thing than most other people. In fact, I would go so far as to say that most if not all people not only want to be successful, they actually can be. Superstar status lies within the reach of all of us. It's only a question of choosing to pursue the things we're good at. When we do that we will matter in important ways that also matter to us.

Psychologists, probably because it is their nature and they can't help themselves, study virtually anything and everything with even miniscule potential for impacting human beings. Naturally, they have studied self-esteem, and have subdivided it in many different ways. Two of their classifications are helpful at this point in our discussion.

Apparently self-esteem comes in both explicit and implicit forms. I sense your excitement building, so let me hurry on with my discussion. In terms as simple as my complex—and some would say convoluted—mind will allow, there are two levels of self-esteem. Explicit self-esteem is evident in the things we say about ourselves to others, while implicit self-esteem is what we say about ourselves to ourselves when no one else is listening. It should be no surprise that the two views are often not the same. The individual who projects a confident outward self-esteem may, in fact, not really feel the same way internally. Outward expres-

EMPOWERED POSSIBILITIES

sions of positive self-esteem can be a potentially dangerous mask, because they make it difficult for the individual to resolve the real issues in his/her life. In fact, that outspoken, competitive, and workaholic coworker who comes across as overbearing in his/her self-confidence is often masking low self-esteem. But that's a topic for another book. I probably don't know enough to write that book, but I'm sure someone else will or maybe even already has.

This book and this particular chapter are about the importance of feeling good enough about yourself to the extent that you know you matter, make a difference, and are needed in a positive, healthy, and balanced way.

Failure to feel good about yourself carries some significant penalties to the quality of your life in general and your health in particular. I've listed a few of those risks below.

> *You can have incredible success if you simply choose to! Wake up every morning and choose one thing to succeed at—it's OK to start small with a series of small goals.*

- A tendency to become involved in destructive relationships
- Obesity
- Eating disorders such as anorexia nervosa and bulimia
- Withdrawal from society
- Failure to achieve full potential
- Difficulty in making friends
- Depression
- Health risks equally as dangerous as high blood pressure, heart disease, stroke, and cancer
- Higher risk of self-destructive behaviors including suicide
- Alcohol and drug addiction
- Gambling
- Compulsive spending

EMPOWERED POSSIBILITIES

- Promiscuity
- Various forms of criminal behavior

Please don't think that just because I listed these negative results of low self-esteem I'm going to get into their root causes. I do not know enough about psychology nor is it the mission of this book to be a psychological tome. I listed these negative results as compelling and convincing proof that not only is feeling good about yourself okay, it is essential to living your best life. I really don't think that anyone reading this book who is suffering from low self-esteem is at significant risk to become a criminal or a prostitute. But I do think the health and addictive challenges listed above are definite risks that must be dealt with if you don't feel a healthy and balanced level of self-respect.

I have told you that while the primary target population for this book is senior citizens, the principles apply at all ages. Lest you think that somehow your sex, age, or position in life insulates you from the risks of poor self-esteem and lessens the importance of knowing that you matter and make a difference, let me be perfectly clear. Low self-esteem, and all of the risks it entails, can strike you regardless of your age, ethnicity, sex, or socioeconomic status.

If self-esteem is a problem for you, if you are currently feeling unneeded and underappreciated, the following suggestions will possibly help you. To feel better about yourself, consider these tactics:

- Give yourself permission to feel good about you.
- Maintain a running list of your successes and the things you do that you feel good about. Review this list several times a day if necessary.
- Identify your needs and make sure they are met.
- Keep an updated list of your good points.
- Identify the good things in those around you.

EMPOWERED POSSIBILITIES

- Reward yourself when you have done well.
- Eliminate negativity from your life. This might include limiting contact with negative people.
- Practice looking on the bright side. Seek the good and the lessons to be learned in everything that happens to you.
- Honestly analyze your close relationships and restructure, limit, or sever those that are destructive.
- Identify any bad habits you may have and work to eliminate them.

In your quest for self-worth wellness, keep these few points in mind: it's okay to start small. In fact sometimes it's helpful to start by picking just one thing each day that you want to accomplish. Doing this will build your self-confidence, strengthen your ability to overcome any obstacle, and ultimately lead to the self-worth wellness you are looking for. If you haven't experienced it in a while, you will be pleasantly surprised to see how good it feels to know you matter. It is all right to have a good opinion of yourself as long as you recognize and are honest about your flaws. Some of the benefits of good self- esteem are:

1. Increased sense of security, even in strange situations
2. Better relationships
3. Greater confidence in your ability to be successful
4. Fewer feelings of hopelessness, guilt, and shame
5. More positive assertiveness in expressing your needs and opinions
6. Increased confidence in the quality of your decisions
7. More realistic and less critical assessment of yourself and others
8. Increased resilience and greater ability to face challenges
9. Better mental health
10. Greater ability to benefit from a growth-based relationship with your God

EMPOWERED POSSIBILITIES

Keep in mind that an honest expression of your self-esteem is not bragging, unless of course you do it in an offensive way. It is about respecting and liking yourself as a total package, gifted with strengths and tempered with weaknesses and flaws.

Oliver Cromwell is a powerful figure in the annals of British history. In his day it was common for important people to have their portraits painted. There were no cameras, so a skilled portrait painter was in high demand. Not only did a good portrait assure a form of immortality, it was also widely used as an opportunity to literally put your best face forward for the benefit of history. If you had facial flaws and other physical deformities, the wise artist covered them over with perfection. Oliver Cromwell, though a powerful and influential man, was not a good-looking man. His face, as are the faces of most aging men I am discovering, had its fair share of warts and moles.

The artist doing his portrait wanted to perfect his look, but Cromwell would have none of it. He said, "Paint me warts and all." It seems he wanted to give future generations an honest look at the real Oliver Cromwell. Apparently he liked himself well enough to be comfortable with his physical flaws. That should be the goal of each one of us.

People who are truly determined to matter and make a difference at any stage in their life tend to have a clearly defined sense of mission that they constantly work to achieve. They are concerned, you see, about how they will be remembered—about what people say of them. They want, in other words, to leave a positive legacy. A true commitment to mission never goes away, not even when they retire.

The real questions for you to consider at this point are this: Is it even possible to have self-worth wellness without being engaged in activities that affirm your ability to make a positive difference

EMPOWERED POSSIBILITIES

and a worthwhile contribution? Do I still matter if I am not doing things that matter to others? I doubt it. Don't you?

There are some basic human needs at issue here. Everyone needs to

- Know that he/she is cared about
- Feel appreciated
- Feel fulfilled, satisfied, and with strong reason to exist
- Feel responded to and listened to
- Know they can continue contributing and making a difference
- Know that he/she is needed

Can any of these needs be met without some positive effort on your part? Again, I don't think so.

If you don't feel appreciated, if you think that nobody cares, if you suspect that no one is listening to you, if you feel unnecessary and pushed to the sidelines of life, could it be because you stopped contributing? Is it possible that you made a choice to drop out of life and now find yourself sidelined and forgotten? If you are needed, there must be a reason why. If you are needed, you are valued and not forgotten. What have you done recently to prove to those around you that they need you?

That being needed is one of the basic human needs may surprise you. With our focus on having our needs met, we often forget that it is just as important and maybe even more so to be needed as it is to have our needs met. Being needed just might be the core factor necessary for self-worth wellness. It certainly is the best possible proof that you matter and can still make a difference in at least one life.

Incidentally, what you do for a living and the things it has allowed you to accumulate are not even remotely accurate measures of your value as a person. Your true value as a person and any rights you may have to positive self-esteem lie solely in your commitment to always give your best and to matter and make a positive difference in the lives of those around you.

Maybe you're in that fortunate position where you feel secure in the knowledge that you are needed, that you matter, your contributions are appreciated, and you make a difference. If so, then you might not need the rest of this chapter. If, however, you would like to be sure that you can matter even more than you currently do, what follows will be helpful.

First, serving others is an excellent way to assure that you are making a difference, and service brings with it some significant health benefits. People who perform useful and selfless service for others report much less stress and fewer health problems. Imagine that!! Serve others, and feel better for it. It just may be that service and a balanced spirit of volunteerism are essential elements of really feeling well.

Additionally, focusing on service can help you recover from great loss, even the death of a spouse or child. One West Coast woman, whose son died from drowning, lived with the knowledge that had her community provided emergency medical services, he very likely would have lived. Determined to make sure no one else suffered a loss like hers and not willing to let her grief define the rest of her life, she became an emergency medical technician, raised the money needed to buy an ambulance, and started the very emergency services that could have saved her son's life. Her efforts have so far saved over one hundred lives. Does she still grieve for her son? Of course, but his death does not define and limit her. She used it as motivation to save others. As painful as losing him has been and continues to be, she has memorialized his death with life-preserving service.

EMPOWERED POSSIBILITIES

Service, in fact, carries such powerful potential for stress reduction and healing that in one study, participants experienced a stronger immune response simply by watching a film on Mother Teresa performing acts of selfless service. Amazing isn't it? They did nothing but watch, and still benefited.

My good friends Rhoda and Paul Layman lost their youngest son to non-Hodgkin's lymphoma at the age of fifteen. Rhoda, one of the most devoted mothers I have known, channeled her grief into ten years of tireless volunteering for the American Cancer society. Does she miss Zac? Of course she does. All of us who knew him do.

I can easily conjure the image of a 15-year-old Zac, just three short months before his death, sitting with my 15-year-old son in the back of my minivan sharing plans for dating and first cars. He was dying but in the process, insisted on living.

> *"The only ones among you who will be really happy are those who will have sought and found how to serve."*
>
> Dr. Albert Schweitzer

Rhoda keeps a bedroom in their home in his honor. It's not a shrine. It's actually a guest room, but it keeps his memory alive and in subtle ways, introduces his spirit and energy to many that never knew him. When his older brother Ben married a few years ago, Zac was present in the form of a burning candle standing in best man position where he would have been had he lived. The sense of loss never leaves, but a life of service built the finest memorial possible to a really fine and hugely entertaining kid.

The best service is rooted in a deep sense of personal mission and purpose. Gordon Miller, a retired banker with only months to live as a result of a losing battle with brain cancer, made it his mission to write a book about a new, more sensible, and much safer way of investing. Here is what a close friend of his, Mr. Davis, said of the impact writing his book had on him:

EMPOWERED POSSIBILITIES

"This book has increased the quality of his life," Mr. Davis said. "And it's given him the knowledge and understanding that if, in fact, the end is near, that the end is not the end."

Banker Miller, when faced with the harsh truth of his impending death, chose not to shroud himself in sorrow, anger, regret, and hopelessness. He chose, rather, to spend his time creating a unique legacy. He chose, as his final act, to use his accumulated knowledge to create wiser investors; and if his friend Mr. Davis read him accurately, it made his life, brief though it may have been, much more satisfying. What will you leave as your legacy?

Civil War hero and two-term President of the United States, Ulysses S. Grant was a great general, a mediocre president, and a horrible businessman. A passionate cigar smoker, General Grant developed a deadly throat cancer when only in his early sixties. Realizing that he had at most a year to live and that his ineffective money handling skills would leave his family destitute, he began a passionate use of the only other exceptional skill besides military prowess that he possessed. General Grant was an excellent writer. Instead of burning what resources he might've had left on searching the world for a cure, he accepted his fate and set about the task of securing his family's future.

He finished his book barely two weeks before his death, and it was a bestseller—more than making up for decades of bad business decisions. Consequently, we remember him as possibly the greatest general ever produced in the United States, an OK president, and an exceptional writer who provided well for his family. His brilliance as a general saved his country. For most, that would have been legacy enough. His skill as a writer and his dogged determination in the face of his own rapidly approaching death secured his family, and that's what, in the end, General Grant cared about the most.

EMPOWERED POSSIBILITIES

You're really never too young to plan for the type of legacy you want to leave behind. If you are working from a sense of mission, and I hope you are, your legacy apart from any money or property you may accumulate will rest on how completely you live your mission and how much it was valued and appreciated.

Sometimes the problem is one of perspective. If you are still working or actively involved as a volunteer, consider this. Some statistics suggest that only one in five persons in the workforce really like their jobs. That's a very sad situation for a lifelong career, but I also suspect that many volunteers are less than satisfied with what they're doing. That would be even sadder, since volunteerism is almost surely and completely a choice.

One of the best bookkeepers I've ever worked with retired just this week. Recently we spoke about career choices and how and why we end up doing what we do. "I wonder," She asked, "if we choose our careers and then learn to like and be good at them, or do we choose them because of what we like and are good at?"

I think it happens both ways, but I truly believe it is far better if our choice is based on natural talents and preferences with built-in ability to acquire the skills necessary to excel. You are more likely to make a difference and leave a better legacy if you spend your time doing what you are passionate about, naturally talented for, and ultimately good at.

Sometimes, in order to be sure that we matter and can make a difference, we have to look for the deeper significance in what we're doing. Simply put, find an activity you can feel passionate about and focus all your years of training and experience on doing that activity with maximum quality and commitment. Stay in touch with the higher purpose of whatever you choose to do. I can illustrate this last point quite effectively with a brief story

EMPOWERED POSSIBILITIES

about a very memorable shoeshine I enjoyed in Columbus, Ohio, in 1995.

I was in town to do a seminar scheduled for the next day and felt the need of a shiny pair of shoes to wear. Fortunately for me, the hotel featured a shoeshine booth, which just happened to be open as I walked by.

As the shoe shiner mounted his chair, it was readily apparent that this wasn't going to be an ordinary shoeshine. This guy was different. In the act of applying the paste to my shoes, he paused and looking up at me asked, "Do you know what I'm really doing here? You probably think I'm just giving you a shoeshine. But I'm not. I'm giving you a foot massage."

With that confident introduction, and using his bare hands to apply the polish, he showed me how the otherwise simple act of putting polish on my shoes could transform into a very pleasant foot massage. He said it made his shoe shines memorable. Anyone could give a shoeshine, but very few would be remembered for their foot massage.

Thanks to his unique approach, he could boast of a tremendous amount of repeat business. Clearly, he'd found the higher calling of shining shoes. If you are caught in what seems to be a dead-end job or volunteer assignment, take a page from his book. Find a higher purpose in what you are doing. Don't just shine shoes; give foot massages. Don't just collect the tolls; practice your stand-up comedy routine. Don't just type invoices; hone your poetic skills by creating rhymes with the names of your accounts. Don't just lay bricks; build cathedrals.

In order to find a higher purpose in any activity, you will need to understand the higher purpose of your life. If you haven't given much thought to what it is you are uniquely talented to do, if you don't have a clear idea of what your life mission and purpose

EMPOWERED POSSIBILITIES

should be, now would be as good a time as any to find out. Often in my seminars, I use my own specially developed personality analysis system to help participants discover their natural talents. If you contact me, I'll guide you through it.

Practically speaking, it's just not possible to find your life mission if you haven't clarified, at least to yourself, what you like to do and are good at, possibly so good at in fact, that hardly anyone you know is as good at and certainly not better. I am concerned at the number of people who seem to feel they have no special talents. For some, it is impossible to claim excellence in anything. Yet when I press them with questions, we always discover at least one thing they do, enjoy doing, and hesitatingly suspect they are better at than most people they know. If you are good at something, give yourself permission to acknowledge that, with appropriate humility of course.

Please, my beloved readers, it is all right to claim your talents. You have permission from the universe to be better at something than anyone else. In fact, my personal belief, after testing literally thousands of people in a variety of professions and walks of life with my system, is that every individual has a set of talents unique enough and strong enough to become a superstar at something. The trick is to find that something.

Earlier I shared with you some starkly disturbing statistics suggesting that as few as 20 percent of all people in the workforce like their jobs enough to feel the joy and satisfaction of living their values and working their mission. Isn't that sad? The only thing sadder is if you are one of them. If you are one of those who don't really care for what they are doing—possibly the next few paragraphs can change your life. It's a six-step process. On the next few pages, you will find worksheets you can use to help you through the process.

EMPOWERED POSSIBILITIES

1. Identify your values.
2. Formalize a brief, written statement of personal mission.
3. Make a list of your most favorite things to do when you are free to choose.
4. List the talents you use when doing those things.
5. Identify volunteer opportunities and even potential careers that require those talents.
6. Make a list of organizations that you feel would value and use your talents and approach them with the offer of your services.

You will find your mission rooted in the things you value. A value is anything you care deeply about and spend significant time and money on. Your values are the most important things in your life. They are the guiding principles that motivate your every waking action. Your values are uniquely yours when you have chosen them freely from the many options that you had. You chose carefully and wisely before making your decision on the cornerstone, foundational beliefs of your life. If you are truly living your values, then they are recognized by those around you in your character, the things you say, and most importantly the things you do.

Your values will determine your life choices, your hobbies, hopefully your career, your health, and how you spend your money. The way you treat your friends, family, business associates, casual contacts, and even your pets are the truest reflection of what you value. Sadly, most people's actions often reveal behaviors vastly inconsistent with the things they might tell others they value.

EMPOWERED POSSIBILITIES

> **My values include:**
>
> 1. _____
>
> 2. _____
>
> 3. _____
>
> 4. _____
>
> 5. _____
>
> 6. _____
>
> 7. _____

Take a moment now and consider the things you value most in life. It might be family. It might be friends. It might even be money. In fact, your values can be anything that you care about so deeply that it is solidly embedded in the foundation for the way you live. List your top values in the spaces provided in the box above.

Your values form the foundation of our personal mission and purpose in life. Your mission is an objective or task that you believe is your calling to carry out. Your mission defines your purpose for being alive and on this planet. Feel free to use the box provided below to record your personal mission statement.

> **My personal life mission is:**
>
> _____
>
> _____
>
> _____
>
> _____

EMPOWERED POSSIBILITIES

With your mission clarified and formalized in writing, consider the things you most enjoy doing. There are no wrong answers to this exercise. We are, after all, focusing on you, so your answers should describe what you enjoy without thought to what others might expect. Your list can include things like traveling, reading, going to movies, entertaining, cooking, baking, serving others, public speaking, working on cars, and/or writing poetry. The choice is completely yours, and in fact it has to be. Who else knows you better than you do? Use the box to the right to complete your answers. Most importantly, keep in mind that it is OK to say you are very good at something. In fact, not only is it OK, it is essential to your sense of well-being.

When I am free to choose, I enjoy doing the following:

1. _____
2. _____
3. _____
4. _____
5. _____
6. _____
7. _____

The next step is an analysis of the list of things you enjoy doing to identify the talents you use when doing them. A talent is, by definition, a natural ability you were born with. Talents only become skills when you use them frequently. Therefore, if you are unsure of just what talents you have, a good place to look is in the things you enjoy doing and are good at. In truth, if you enjoy doing something, even if you are not particularly good at, there is a hidden talent in there somewhere. For example, I like to write and I thoroughly enjoy speaking in public; one of my talents is, therefore, the use of words. I like a good story that makes people laugh; entertainment is one of my talents. But enough about me; what about you?

EMPOWERED POSSIBILITIES

If you enjoy doing things for others, it is likely that service is a talent. If your hobby is working on cars, mechanical reasoning is a talent. My friend Jim, a highly successful businessman, has a passion for restoring antique cars. Precision, patience, and attention to detail are clearly in his list of talents. Mark loves to cook, host parties, and work on computers. What do you think he would say his talents are? What are your talents? They are embodied in the things you have said you enjoy, so look for them, identify them, and list them in the table to the right.

The things I am enjoy doing suggest that my talents include:

1. _____
2. _____
3. _____
4. _____
5. _____
6. _____
7. _____

With your talents identified and formalized in writing, it's time to consider potential career and/or volunteer opportunities that would use and value your personal and unique set of talents. Remember, you will be happiest and most successful when you affiliate with organizations that share and appreciate your values and sense of mission and can put your best talents to good and regular use. Use the box on the left to record your answers.

Organizations that I would fit well with include:

1. _____
2. _____
3. _____
4. _____
5. _____

At this point a little practice should prove helpful. On the next page you will find the values and mission statements for my company, Waterman Communities, Inc. Additionally, included is a listing of talents we feel are necessary for maximum

EMPOWERED POSSIBILITIES

success in our organization, both as a member of the staff and as a resident in one of our communities.

For purposes of learning, compare your personal values and mission statement and your list of talents to those of Waterman Communities, Inc. How well would you fit in?

A key point to be made about the importance of values and a mission is that in order for you to be truly involved and engaged in satisfying ways, you need a connection to an organization with values and a mission that closely match yours. You can't and won't give your best to an organization you don't believe in.

Of course, once you've clarified your values and mission and have identified the organization you'd like to be involved with, you have to find things within that organization that will allow you to contribute according to your best and most preferred talents.

> *Waterman Communities Core Values Are:*
>
> 1. *Integrity*
> 2. *Professionalism*
> 3. *Wellness*
> 4. *Community*
> 5. *Caring*
> 6. *Security*

In identifying your personal values and mission, be very sure that they are really yours and not the dreams held for you by influential family and friends. You cannot truly be happy and satisfied in a job where the tasks, duties, mission, and rewards don't fit you. In fact, if you don't really love what you do and can't say you are using your best and most preferred talents most of the time, it is very unlikely that you are performing to your maximum potential. And even if by some miracle you get to be good at it, I doubt that your level of performance is as good as it could be if you were doing something you truly enjoyed and cared about. Let me share a sad story with you.

EMPOWERED POSSIBILITIES

Some years back while working as a consultant in a nursing home in the Orlando, Florida, area, I met a young orderly who shared his goal to be a doctor. As he said those words I searched his face for some sense of enthusiasm or excitement, but there was no such evidence. He stated his career goal in such a dry, matter-of-fact way that I simply could not believe he really meant it. But he did. Being a doctor was what he was going to do for a career and that was that. However, after further questioning, he admitted that the goal was his father's, not his.

> Waterman Communities Mission Statement:
>
> *To empower the ability of residents and staff to age successfully living their best life in an atmosphere of home, family, community and wellness*

He was going to be a doctor for no better reason than that his father expected him to. There was no love of medicine; no excitement at the prospect of healing; only bored, somewhat despondent resignation to his father's will.

I have not seen the young man since that day. I don't know if he ended up a doctor. I rather hope he didn't, however, for I believe it takes passion to make a good doctor or a good anything for that matter. I don't think I would like to have as my doctor, an individual who chose medicine to please his father and not himself. By the same token, if you truly wish to matter and make a difference in the areas in which you choose to get involved, be sure you pick things you care about and are truly passionate for.

Certainly the British rock group, The Zimmers, introduced to you in the last chapter, matter and are making a significant difference in the perception society has of older people. If you don't believe me, check them out on YouTube. The name Zimmers, by the way, shows their sense of humor about what they do. The Zimmer is an assistive walking device used primarily by old people to

EMPOWERED POSSIBILITIES

avoid falling as they walk. In the United States they are known as walkers. The symbolism there is pretty deep but quite effective if you think about it long enough.

Bill, one of my personal heroes, just passed his ninetieth birthday. It's not unusual for me to see Bill around my office several times a week. He comes for three reasons. First, I think he likes the hugs my assistant, Betty, has waiting for him. Secondly, I know he likes his favorite candy, which Betty makes sure is available in the candy dish by the door. But third, and most importantly I believe, Bill comes to debate with and offer advice to our CFO and sometimes me. As chairman of our resident finance advisory committee, Bill has made it his personal mission to develop and share as many ideas for improving our financial performance as he can conjure.

> In a Waterman Community, Individuals Who Excel at Living Their Best Life, Whether as Staff or Residents, Use the Following Talents to Do So:
>
> 1. Engagement
> 2. Service
> 3. Optimism
> 4. Dependability
> 5. Willingness to learn
> 6. Friendship
> 7. Spirituality
> 8. Openness to new ideas and adventure
> 9. Commitment
> 10. Accuracy

He has initiated and coordinated no fewer than ten grant-writing efforts seeking money to fund the further development of our state-of-the-art Alzheimer's program. It's not unusual for both the CFO and me to get a memo and a visit from Bill on the same day. He'd come personally even if there were no candy or hugs because his active mind moves his thoughts to action pretty quickly, and he lacks the patience to wait until his ideas make it to us through our interdepartmental mail delivery system.

EMPOWERED POSSIBILITIES

We have found through the years that Bill is well worth listening to. During his career, he managed his company well enough to retire at the early age of fifty-five. Even then, nearly forty years ago, he was astute enough to realize that he shouldn't simply retire to a life of ease and doing nothing. At best he should retread. Consequently, he went into real estate development with his sons.

> *Whatever you are, be a good one*
> Abraham Lincoln

Knowing and working with Bill brings into sharp focus one of the great losses to our country and its economy. When older people with a lifetime of valuable experience are left to mold and crumble on the sideline, much wisdom is sacrificed. Bill's experience and that of the rest of the members of our finance committee have greatly enhanced our operation. Furthermore, for them, I think it has sharpened their minds and increased their zest for living. They are tougher on us than our own Board of Directors, and are the main reason why our board doesn't find it necessary to establish its own finance committee.

Betty, another one of my senior heroes, has been at our Waterman Village longer than I have, and that means more than seventeen years. Well into her nineties, Betty made it her mission to see that the residents in our community had a decent and appropriate place to meet and worship. She put her money as well as her actions where her mouth is and today remains the donor of the largest charitable gift we've ever received. Due in large part to her generosity, our Garden of Life Fellowship Hall (GOLF Hall for you acronym enthusiasts) exists and is in use every day. Betty determined to make a difference and she has.

> *It's frustrating when you know all the answers but nobody bothers to ask you the questions...*

EMPOWERED POSSIBILITIES

I can't close this discussion on the importance of continuing to matter and make a difference at all ages of your life without admitting that many retired people seem openly proud of the fact that they are retired with no obligations, no interruptions to their day, no one telling them what to do unless of course they are married, and no calendar to keep other than for an increasingly endless string of doctor's appointments. By the way, I'm not so sure they're proud of their volume of doctors' appointments. Oh sure, they seem to like to talk about their physical ailments a lot, but I fear that this is all too often because they've removed themselves from activities that matter—activities that would, in fact, take their mind off their discomforts and that would result in significant improvement to their health. Sadly, some people really don't allow themselves anything else to talk about but their health.

I introduced you to my father in the preceding chapter. In fourteen years of retirement prior to his death, he never found an activity he considered worth engaging in; thus he ultimately doubted his personal worth and ability to contribute. Many years after he died at an age just short of eighty, his youngest brother, my Uncle Leslie, said something very revealing about my father.

"Your dad," he said, "was built to live to be one hundred. I don't think I was, and I don't think our brother Albert was either."

I've asked myself through the years why it was that if dad was built to last to one hundred and uncles Albert and Leslie weren't, why did Leslie make it to eighty-four and Albert to ninety-four, while my dad, supposedly the sturdily constructed one, died at seventy-nine? The answer is Albert and Leslie made sure they had something to do that they considered worth doing. Dad didn't, and it took him those fourteen years to die.

Oh sure, he had some good times along the way. There were brief periods when gardening was important and he did eventually

EMPOWERED POSSIBILITIES

have a small shop to putter in on those increasingly rare occasions when he felt like it. There were also grandchildren and grand nieces and nephews to babysit and regale with stories. But it wasn't music. And music, as I told you, was his passion.

So please make a commitment right now to matter and make a difference. Get involved. Contribute and make sure you leave a positive legacy. Above all, enjoy the satisfaction of knowing you are needed.

The benefits of mattering, contributing, and making a difference include:

- The satisfaction of being useful and needed
- The joy of contributing and making a difference
- The comfort and security that comes from leaving a positive legacy

In a Waterman community, our staff goes out of their way to make sure our residents know that they matter. Opportunities to make a difference through committee involvement are widely available. In recognition that all of our residents have been successful at something in their lives, we encourage our staff to ask for advice but not for money. What better way to affirm an older individual's value as a person and their continued ability to contribute and make a difference then to ask them for advice and guidance?

We want our staff and residents to be friends. It is an inescapable fact that just as our residents need our staff, our staff also need our residents.

Some years ago, a nursing assistant shared a highly insightful comment with me. When asked why she liked her, job her answer was, "I like coming in every day because I know that when I do, I will get love."

EMPOWERED POSSIBILITIES

Isn't that beautiful? That Kentucky nursing assistant knew that she needed the love of her residents as badly as they needed her loving services. Isn't that really what life is all about-people helping people, people making a difference in the lives of those around them?

> We must become the change we want to see.
>
> *You may never know what results come of your action, but if you do nothing there will be no result.*
>
> **Mahatma Gandhi**

Incidentally, in your often alternating roles as customer and consumer, you might remember that good service is a two way street. As much as you want and need respect and good service, those serving you want and need respect and appreciation. How often, I wonder, is the poor service and disrespect we experience in direct proportion to the respect and appreciation we give?

Determine to matter and make a difference. It will add quality and quantity to your life. It is an important element in empowering your ability to age successfully and live your personal best life.

Before continuing on to the next chapter, take a moment to review the table on the next page. On it you will find a list of tactics covered in this chapter for improving your sense of self-worth. Study the list carefully, and then in the space to the left of each tactic, enter a date by which **you propose to implement that tactic in your life**.

EMPOWERED POSSIBILITIES

MY SELF-WORTH WELLNESS IMPROVEMENT PLAN	
DATE	SELF-WORTH WELLNESS IMPROVEMENT TACTICS
	Develop a clear statement of your natural and most preferred skills, talents, abilities and preferences.
	Identify the things you value most in life.
	Develop a written statement of mission and purpose for yourself.
	Make a comprehensive list of everything about you that you feel defines your value as a person being sure to indicate why for each item on the list.
	Develop a list of people in your life who are better off because of you and be sure to list how and why.
	Assemble a list of peple who would benefit by greater, positive involvement with you and strategize on how to make that involvement happen.
	Determine to show your appreciation to the most special people in your life in ways that are meaningful to them at least once per day.
	Involve yourself in activities that are personally meaningful to you based on your natural talents and your mission and purpose.
	Serve others completely without expectation of reward in order to enjoy being needed for the purest of reasons.
	Determine to make a positive difference in everything you do.
	Assure that your legacy is intact and will be what you want it to be.
	Regularly reafirm your personal value and worth.
	Make sure that you have someone to love and at least one person who loves you back.
	Always make sure you have something in your future worth looking forward to.

CHAPTER 5:
PHYSICAL WELLNESS:
PRESERVE YOUR PHYSICAL FITNESS

Around about the age of forty, the human body begins to lose muscle strength. As much as I would prefer it not to be true, this is a natural part of the aging process; natural, that is, if you allow it to be. Loss of strength may be a natural part of the aging process, but it certainly isn't an essential one. In fact, loss of strength is only the beginning of losses typically blamed on the aging process. On the next page you will find a table listing fifteen things that happen as we age. Just because these things commonly happen doesn't mean that there is little or nothing to be done about preventing or at least mitigating their effects. Other than deteriorating hearing and vision and loss of hair, you can greatly reduce the impact of all the rest by practicing the principles outlined in this book. You will be well on your way to agreement by the time you finish this chapter. And by the way, if there was a foolproof, cost-effective way to make thinning hair thicken again, not only would I tell you, I'd be doing it.

> **Physically fit:**
>
> 1. ***The general condition of the body or mind with reference to soundness and vigor: good health; poor health.***
>
> 2. ***Soundness of body or mind; freedom from disease or ailment: to have one's health.***
>
> 3. ***Vigor and vitality***

EMPOWERED POSSIBILITIES

Probably the most obvious element of wellness is physical fitness. In our youth touting society, much is made of staying fit. Yet obesity is a national problem of embarrassing proportions, no pun intended, and few physical challenges pose greater threat to good health than obesity.

Before we get too deeply involved in a discussion on physical fitness, I'd like to make what I consider to be the most important points first. To be physically fit requires physical strength, stamina, balance, and flexibility. It is these four things that are most often allowed to deteriorate during the aging process.

By the end of this chapter, I believe you'll be convinced

> *Commonly Perceived Effects of Aging Include*
>
> - *Weakening vision starting as early as age ten*
> - *Loss of muscle strength and coordination starting at age thirty*
> - *Deterioration of heart and blood vessels after age forty*
> - *Decline in learning ability after age fifty*
> - *Beginning at age thirty, loss in height of 1/16 inch per year*
> - *Accumulation of body fat around hips and thighs*
> - *Loss of scalp hair, primarily in men*
> - *Skin becomes less elastic, develops age spots, and moles and warts appear*
> - *Wounds take longer to heal*
> - *Decline in efficiency of heart, lungs, and kidneys*
> - *Loss of hearing*
> - *Decline in ability to taste*
> - *Mental confusion and memory loss*
> - *Become more accident prone*
> - *Weakening immune system*
> - *Metabolism slows down*

that this deterioration does not have to happen, certainly, at least, to the degree to which it usually does. In fact, it is more likely that any loss of strength and agility is due to inactivity than it is an essential result of the aging process. You can build muscle mass, maintain and even improve your stamina, and increase your balance and flexibility even as you age. All it takes is a firm commitment, a sensible plan, and a carefully balanced approach.

> *Body Mass Index (BMI), a way to measure what proportion of your body weight is fat, is a valuable predictor of your ability to age successfully. Studies suggest that a BMI in the range of 21 to 22 is best for your health. Use the following formula to calculate your own BMI:*
>
> *Your weight in pounds ____ / 2.2 =*
>
> *Your weight in Kilograms ____;*
>
> *Your height in inches ____ X .0254 =*
>
> *Your height in meters ____ squared = ____;*
>
> *Your weight in kilograms ____ /*
>
> *Your height in meters squared ____ =*
>
> *Your BMI ____.*

Perhaps you need an epiphany moment of clarity. Mine came in the dining room of the Waterman Village Lodge about five years ago. I walked up behind a colleague of approximately my age, and as is often my custom, clapped him on the back. As I did, I felt what seemed like his entire body jiggle, much as Jell-O jiggles at the slightest jarring or touch.

Right then I made myself a promise. That will not be me. Since that day, I've been on a mission to keep my own personal jiggle factor down. Join me as I conduct a brief tour of my sometimes-sporadic journey towards jiggle-free physical fitness.

EMPOWERED POSSIBILITIES

I have been a fairly faithful member of a fitness gym since shortly after my fiftieth birthday in 1997. During my time as a member, I have seen many new members come and often quickly go, particularly in the month of January. It seems that some of those New Year's resolutions prove difficult to live up to. What you see is the big bang/quick fizzle evolution of exercise phenomenon. The most extreme example of this I've ever seen however, happened one morning at the Bally Fitness Center in Altamonte Springs, Florida, a facility that is now, alas, a generic furniture store.

I was working out on one of my machines when I heard the man next to me sigh and say, "Where did it go?"

"Where did what go?" I asked.

"My youth," he replied.

As I looked at him, I could see that his physique, though bloated and flabby now, had once been toned and muscular. The outline of his youthful Adonis was still visible even if only barely. From the amount he was attempting to lift I could tell that he had once pushed some pretty heavy weights. That he wanted his body back was obvious. That he was trying too hard soon became apparent when he let the weights down with a clatter, emitted a loud sigh, got up, and walked out the door. I never saw him again. He was in and out in one day. Most New Year's resolution motivated fitness wannabes last at least a week before they drop out. For this man, however, the magnitude of his fall from physical fitness was so vast that he couldn't face the long journey back.

The lesson for you in the experience of this unhappy man is to start at a sensible level and work your way up, slowly if necessary. It doesn't matter how strong you once were. What matters is how strong you can be if you are patient, persistent, and sensible.

EMPOWERED POSSIBILITIES

My friend Virgil is a much better example for you. The other morning I saw him working out on one of my favorite machines. It is a machine on which I easily handle 90 to 110 pounds. Virgil was lifting 30. I gave him a hard time, but he put me in my place when he said, "Hey, 30 pounds is pretty good. I started at 10."

Accomplishment is a relative concept best measured from your own personal starting point. That's your starting point by the way, and no one else's.

To make my case for physical fitness, I'd like to hold myself out as an example. Unfortunately, if you could see me now you might have trouble interpreting just what great shape I'm in.

> *Physical Wellness: Preserve and promote physical fitness through a balanced program of exercise, restoration, and nutrition.*

I'm sixty-four years old, 5'10" tall, and I weigh 215 pounds. I told you in an earlier chapter that I have just recently joined a martial arts class. More specifically I have taken up the Israeli hand-to-hand combat program, Krav Maga. I go two nights a week and the workouts are quite intense. I'm the oldest member of the class by a good ten years, but I am not the weakest or the slowest. For the most part, I keep up and I'm having a great time. As overweight as I am, I can do 340 repetitions running in place and up to 170 jumping jacks, all without stopping and in the space of five minutes. I clearly didn't start at that level. It has taken nearly three months to work up to it. I've done as many as twenty-four push-ups in my first set; when I started, I struggled to make eight.

My Krav Maga class is in addition to my program at Gold's Gym, where I focus on strength training and aerobic exercise. On one machine where I press 90 pounds twelve times each for three sets, I barely made it to nine repetitions at 50 pounds for one set when I started three years ago.

EMPOWERED POSSIBILITIES

Keep in mind: I've made these gains above the age of sixty. Since my history shows that I've dabbled with physical fitness at the beginning of each of the last four decades of my life, I can tell you that the older I get, the longer it seems to take and the more persistently determined I have to be. It is inescapably true: the younger you are when you start, the better. But being old should never be used as an excuse not to start a physical fitness improvement program. Let me share with you my journey.

The decades of my life have flown by at warp speed. It doesn't seem so long ago that I was twenty-nine teetering on the brink of thirty. That seemed to me a good time to get in shape, but when it came right down to it, I decided without much trouble that I wasn't in such bad shape anyway, so I changed little. In my late thirties, I made the commitment to get in shape by the time I turned forty. When I did turn forty, a quick survey of my body parts suggested that I still wasn't in such bad shape, and besides, forty wasn't that old. I still had plenty of time. So, aside from fairly regular early-morning walks, I didn't do much to improve.

As fifty approached, however, I knew I had to do something. After all, I weighed in at 187 pounds, well above my target weight of 170. This time, to think was to act, and I joined a Bally Fitness Center.

Faithfully for six months, I was a regular early-morning moving and sweating fixture at Bally's Apopka, Florida, location. During those six months, I studiously avoided my bathroom scale. But the day came when I felt good enough about my progress that confidently, I mounted it, fully expecting to see a significant weight loss. I saw instead that I had gained 10 pounds. My starting point of 187 pounds, which had once caused me so much concern, now ballooned to 197 pounds. Clearly I was heading the wrong way. Oh yes, I took some comfort in the illogical folk wisdom that muscle weighs more than fat, but 10 pounds is still 10 pounds. Ultimately, I needed a combination of continued exercise and

EMPOWERED POSSIBILITIES

a serious diet. Today, by the way, such is my improvement in stamina and muscle that my current goal is a return to the 187 I started with nearly fifteen years ago. Life can, indeed, be a cycle of circles.

Now, if your memory is sharp, and I trust that it is, you are remembering that just a few paragraphs ago I told you I weighed 215 pounds. Sadly, that is true. For almost as soon as I lost the weight, I began putting it back on. I continued exercising, but chocolate cake found its way back onto my plate as did the occasional delectable scoop of ice cream. As you probably know, weight control can be an endless battle, but a battle well worth waging.

For me, my sixties are a new day. I'm a member of a new gym. I'm attending vigorous martial arts classes. I'm even enduring weekly doses of acupuncture for heaven's sake. But most importantly, I am convinced of the kind of seventy-year-old I want to be. And to be that kind of seventy-year-old, I only have my sixties to prepare. I can't go back in time, and neither can you. We can only move forward and make the most of what we have in our futures.

Preserving and enhancing physical fitness requires activity, exercise, and nutritional balance. For older people, an often-overlooked but incredibly vital aspect of physical fitness is improving your balance as you walk. Yes folks, I am telling you that, barring physical disability, an unsteady walking gait does not have to be part of the aging process. By the way, even with a disability, your balance can usually be improved. Your balance can be and should be improved, and here's why:

Falls are a leading cause of injury, often leading to death for people at any age but particularly older people. Poor balance, while not always the sole culprit is one of the most dangerous factors. Without good balance, a debilitating fall is shockingly easy.

EMPOWERED POSSIBILITIES

A commonly accepted truth about aging is that our bones get weaker and are more easily broken. As with so many of the facts of aging we discuss in this book, this statement, too, is true if we let it be. An added benefit of exercise is that it makes our bones sturdier and therefore less likely to break even if we fall. I asked my good friend and favorite chiropractor to comment on this. This is what she had to say:

> **The Myth:** Growing weaker is a natural and unavoidable consequence of aging. **The Facts:** It takes work, but you can increase your strength, flexibility, and physical capability at literally any age.

"There is a powerful law in the body called Wolff's Law, and it applies to our bones. It says that any time we put pressure on an area of bone, it grows. In today's sedentary lifestyle, we are not tapping into the body's ability to develop new bone structure. Bones are living tissues. If we don't stay active, our bones become brittle and weak.

"If weakening our bone structure were all the mischief inactivity caused, it would be bad enough; but sadly there is more. When we allow our bones to become brittle and weakened by a sedentary lifestyle, it results in poor posture. Poor posture distorts the body, reducing our lung capacity, decreasing our range of motion, and obstructing the flow of oxygen and blood to the brain."

Thank you, Dr. Ramah. Carrying these thoughts a few steps further, it strikes me that when we limit our exercise out of fear of falling, we are in fact weakening our muscles, bones, and brains even further, thus increasing the risk of the very thing we seek—with inactivity—to prevent.

Another contributing cause of falls is failure to avoid tripping hazards due to poor eyesight. And it doesn't help that often, poor nutritional habits lead to exceptionally brittle and therefore easily breakable bones.

EMPOWERED POSSIBILITIES

With these thoughts in mind, it only makes sense that an effective fitness program should include, along with the traditional muscle-building and aerobic exercises, balance training. To illustrate the importance of good balance when walking, I recently heard that the most dependable predictor of the ability of an eighty-five-year-old to live long enough to be a healthy ninety-year-old is the steadiness of his or her walking gait. Wouldn't it be nice not to have to worry about a fall?

A few weeks ago, my good friend Vic stopped by my office for a visit. Vic is approaching his ninetieth birthday with mixed emotions. Most days he's happy to be alive. On bad days, however, he questions why he's still alive. On this particular day, Vic was in a pretty good mood. We had a fine time laughing and joking as we usually do.

Recently I'd noticed in Vic an increased tendency to shuffle as he walks. He'd noticed it too and blamed it on the lack of leather-soled shoes in styles that he likes. For a guy who loved to dance, this was not a good thing.

Our conversation finished, and Vic turned to go. As I watched, one of his turning, shuffling feet - almost in slow motion it seemed caught on the carpet and down he went, breaking his hip. It happened so fast and his fall was so smooth, I had difficulty believing him when he said his hip was broken.

Today Vic is rehabilitating nicely. I visited him in his home a few days ago. He's still receiving therapy and his walking is improving. He tells me he'll be going to the New Year's Eve dance though he may not try dancing this year. So what can we learn from Vic's unfortunate experience?

I believe there are at least three reasons for his fall. One is his shuffling gait; two, the rubber soles of his shoes which do not slide well when he shuffles, and three, his shaky balance. He's

EMPOWERED POSSIBILITIES

turning ninety in a few days and seems determined to get his walk and just maybe even his dance step back. For Vic, better balance and a steady, more confident gait will be the determining factors. I think he'll do it, because he wants to and believes he can.

If you aren't yet convinced that starting an exercise program even if you are old in numbers of years is a good idea, consider the following.

Research shows that the human body can develop new muscle fiber up to about the age of eighty. Beyond the age of eighty, you may not be developing new muscle fiber, but regular exercise can and will make the muscle fiber you've already developed grow. In effect, you never get too old to grow stronger. Anyone, regardless of his or her physical condition, can profit from exercise. Your body has amazing capacity to heal and restore itself. All it needs is the opportunity, and you control that.

This past summer my friend Duke lost his constant and years long battle to survive his many disabilities. But what a fight he put up for more years than I bothered to count. Duke was eighty-five when he died and in the years I knew him, he went through several similar cycles.

> **Time may be a great healer but it is a lousy beautician. Fortunately, wrinkles, warts, and age spots don't hurt.**

First he would get sick, so sick that many feared he was dying; many, that is, but not Duke. Three times he fought his way back from serious, bedbound illness and at least two lengthy stays in our nursing home, to a faithful return to the treadmill in our fitness center. The thing I haven't told you about Duke that makes his story and his determination even more remarkable is that it had been years since Duke was able to eat

EMPOWERED POSSIBILITIES

food in the normal and enjoyable way. Thanks to some unfortunate earlier life choices, his nourishment could only come through a tube. But that didn't stop him. He persisted in his battle against illness and overcame three times against tremendous odds. Even his losing fourth fight was a brave and bold one. It wasn't in Duke's nature to give up. I cannot imagine what it would be like to spend the last ten years of my life without even a taste of my favorite foods.

Then, there is Jim. These days, Jim needs a walker to maintain his balance, and his bout with arthritis has left his once 6'6" frame a bent, bowed, and slightly twisted 5'10". Every day, however, Jim makes his way to the fitness center. Once there, he makes the rounds of his favorite machines. Jim is acutely aware of his physical limitations and is very careful to pace himself. He has a system, and he follows it faithfully.

In addition to exercise, Jim loves to read. Fortunately for Jim, our library is located just across the hall from the fitness center. Jim's pattern is to work a couple machines, and then retire to the library for a good book. Once refreshed, Jim returns to the fitness center for a couple more machines. It sometimes takes him two hours to finish all the machines he likes to use, but he sticks with it until he's done, and his efforts have paid off. As my friend Greg puts it, Jim has a real set of guns on him. I am more than twenty years younger than Jim and I'd be pleased if my muscles had as much definition as his do.

If walking is your exercise of choice, consider doing it outside. As you walk, pay attention to the things around you. Notice the variety of landscaping patterns. Check out the kind of cars people drive. Count the number of for sale signs. Relish the occasional sprints made necessary by the barking interest of neighborhood dogs. In doing these things as you walk, you will be increasing your knowledge of your neighborhood and in the process, stimulating your brain.

EMPOWERED POSSIBILITIES

If in your walk, you come to an obstacle such as a fallen tree, consider climbing over it instead of going around it. In this way you will be improving your balance and thereby reducing your risk of falling. If your walking is confined to a treadmill, use the time to strengthen your brain. Watch TV, listen to the radio or your iPod, or read. As you will learn in a later chapter, the connection between physical exercise and your ability to think clearly and reason effectively is striking and essential.

Another often-overlooked aspect of physical fitness is restoration. No matter how much you may enjoy the physical activity you are involved in, your muscles do need time to restore and strengthen. When on the job, take your breaks. Alter the flow of your life with regular vacations.

Surprisingly, research has shown that people who take regular breaks and vacations are up to 10 percent more productive than people who do not. Yet how often do we hear people say, "I was so busy today I didn't even get a minute's break"? If you were to tell them that they would have gotten more done by changing pace with a break, they probably wouldn't believe you. Isn't that sad?

Amazing, isn't it, that people who do not take breaks during the course of the workday, use as their excuse, the need to get everything done—when in fact, they'd get more done by taking their breaks? If you don't get anything else out of this book, I hope I've made this point well. If you really want to get more done, take breaks to restore your energy and sharpen your focus. You'll feel better and your boss, if you have one, will be amazed at how much more you get done. Let's turn now to a brief discussion on the importance of muscle flexibility.

The best way to increase muscle flexibility is by stretching. Regular stretching of your muscles is a good thing, but before you start, remember this. Recent research shows that you need to warm

EMPOWERED POSSIBILITIES

Punching Dummy Bob is no match for Dale's lightning jabs!!!

your body muscles up before you stretch. I know that's counter intuitive to what you've probably been taught all these years. You probably believe, as did I, that you should stretch your muscles before you use them. Now we know that it is important to do some basic warm-up exercises before stretching. As an example, my Krav Maga instructor prepares our class for stretching with five minutes of running in place and jumping jack exercises. I hate jumping jacks by the way—always have and always will—but I probably won't mention that to my instructor.

Let me share with you a bit of my own personal journey toward increased flexibility. For the past several years I have noted an increased difficulty getting out of my sedan. My SUV, because it sits higher, is not a problem. Further, if I needed to pick up something from the floor or just bend down to tie my shoes, I encountered a struggle.

You could say, and I admit that it would be fair, that part of my difficulty is in overcoming the obstacle I have placed in my own way through the years—my round, and I say this proudly, basically firm belly. My belly may be big; it certainly is larger than I wish it was; but the jiggle factor is very, very low. But I digress.

In any event, lack of flexibility, particularly in my knees, calves, and hamstrings, made bending and squatting difficult. I could only get my knees to squat at a slightly better than 90-degree angle. This became a real problem when I took up Krav Maga.

EMPOWERED POSSIBILITIES

Thanks to my days as a workplace injury prevention consultant, I know quite a bit about how muscle strains happen, and lack of flexibility is the major culprit. If my plan was to engage in hand-to-hand combat where the potential for injury was high, I needed to do whatever I could to reduce my risk. Clearly that meant I needed more flexibility.

To that end, I began a series of treatments with my now good friend Dr. Wang. After receiving a combination of acupuncture, deep tissue therapy, and aggressive muscle massage, I can now squat almost as well as I could at the age of twenty. I won't tell you that my squatting is completely without pain, but I will say that the pain has mostly gone away. He tells me that I still need to improve my muscle flexibility, but that my knees are now just fine. I need to massage my legs on a daily basis and practice my stretching and squatting several times during the day.

The rewards for me have proven tremendous. Not only can I squat with relative comfort to pick things up from the floor and tie my shoes, but I get up from chairs more easily as well. Stepping up and out of my low-lying sedan is now as easy as jumping down from my SUV. I'm walking faster. I can now chase the dog until she gets tired. I'm most grateful of all, however, for the fact that my feet don't hurt as much. If it can work for me, and remember that my muscles have to raise and lower an extra thirty to forty pounds, it can certainly work for you.

Oh yes, I almost forgot. I spend a lot of time at the computer and as a result, often experience neck and shoulder discomfort. Dr. Wang taught me that the strain results from hunching forward as I type. The antidote: periodically straighten up, lean back, raise my arms, and stretch backwards. In this way, I am providing my body with movements counter to the ones that create the strain, and I feel much better as a result, even after hours at the computer.

EMPOWERED POSSIBILITIES

By the way, I am currently considering a surprising possibility. I may not, in fact, be overweight. A few weeks ago I found myself in my doctor's exam room with some time on my hands. Looking for something to do while I waited my turn, I idly traced down the columns of the weight chart posted on the wall, looking for my weight. When I found it, and without really giving it much thought, I traced over to the height column, totally unsuspecting of the emerging revelation coming my way. The height associated with my weight was 6'5". It took a moment, but it hit me with the force of a falling rock. I'm 6'5" tall!!! Looking down I realized it's just that my height isn't linear in the way height usually is. It is more ovate. I'm still not fully decided yet, but I am strongly leaning toward my new height theory.

This revelation has brought me little comfort however. My dilemma now is this. Do I stay heavy at 6'5," of non-linear height—as a child I always wanted to be that tall—or do I diet back down to 5'10" and a weight of around 180 pounds? What do you think? I could use some advice.

Oh well, let me reiterate some key points. Physical fitness is vital to your ability to enjoy to the max whatever your future holds. Achieving and maintaining physical fitness is a never ending challenge, and at times, with progress that all too often looks like failure. Remember those unexpected ten pounds I gained when I started my fitness program at the gym? That felt to me like failure, but I altered my approach and pressed forward. Tough as it is, achieving physical fitness is a more than worthy goal. Now, let's take a look at some of the rewards and payoffs of physical fitness. Remember as you read them: these payoffs can be yours at some level no matter your age.

The payoffs of physical fitness include

- Higher energy levels
- Less sickness

EMPOWERED POSSIBILITIES

- Increased capacity to do more of the things you enjoy
- More productivity
- You'll be a smoking hot babe or stud magnet even if your age designates you senior status
- Your friends and family will be amazed at the things you'll be able to do
- It'll do wonders for your self-esteem
- And finally, very simply, your life will be far more fun

Another piece of the fitness puzzle is proper nutrition. There are eight key nutritional challenges that come as part of the aging process. Fortunately, all eight can be addressed with a balanced diet and the right kinds and amounts of exercise. In fact, most experts on aging agree that with a proper diet, few if any nutritional supplements should be needed. Sadly there is a growing body of evidence that suggests that most of the avalanche of anti-aging products, bombarding our senses at every turn, make promises they simply can't keep. Advertising hype aside, scientific evidence is clear. Eating the right foods makes a distinct and positive improvement in your health. The best that can be said for most supplements is, they don't seem to hurt. Now, let's take a quick look at those eight key nutritional challenges found in the aging process.

Nutritional Challenge Number One: As we age, our metabolism—the rate at which the body converts food to energy—slows down. It doesn't take a rocket scientist to figure out that if our body is burning its food-generated fuel at a slower rate, we are risking weight gain and all of the problems that come with it. If our consumption of food remains constant while its conversion to energy declines, weight gain is inevitable.

Fortunately there are some things we can do to combat this natural aging phenomena. We can increase our metabolism and burn more calories by:

- Increasing physical exercise
- Using resistance training to strengthen muscles and build muscle mass
- Adjusting our diet to include more whole grains, fruits and vegetables, lean protein, and nonfat or low-fat dairy
- Practicing moderation in what we eat

Nutritional Challenge Number Two: As the need for calories declines, the need for protein remains the same: 45 to 60 grams per day for the average adult. Consequently, reducing our food consumption to avoid weight gain brings with it the risk of protein deficiency. After all, adequate protein is essential for the growth, repair, and maintenance of healthy tissue. Fortunately, this is a relatively easy challenge to meet with proper menu planning. We can

- Include adequate protein in each meal to ensure that over the course of the day the requisite 45 to 60 grams are consumed
- Choose high-quality protein such as fish, poultry, and lean meats
- Include legumes such as lentils and kidney beans
- Include nonfat or low-fat dairy products if dietary preferences and/or restrictions allow

Nutritional Challenge Number Three: The condition of your teeth and gums has a major impact on the body's ability to absorb adequate nutrition. For older adults, the nearly 80 percent risk of periodontal disease combined with the use of dentures prevents the proper chewing of food. According to my longtime dentist and good friend Dr. Mark Offenback, when food is not properly chewed, the saliva, whose job it is to begin the breakdown process of the food in preparation for its ultimate conversion into energy, cannot properly function. Without proper chewing, the body cannot extract maximum nutritional benefit from food.

EMPOWERED POSSIBILITIES

According to Dr. Offenback, replacing the natural teeth with dentures can, by itself, reduce life expectancy by more than five years. Add in periodontal disease, and the situation worsens dramatically. Now, not only will food be improperly chewed, but the discomfort caused by periodontal disease working in illicit tandem with ill-fitting dentures will result in avoidance of harder to chew foods such as fresh fruits, vegetables, and meat.

Who knew that not chewing properly could shorten your life? Maybe you don't wear dentures. Let's even suppose that your gums are healthy and pain-free. Rushing through a meal, wolfing down your food in partially chewed chunks, also inhibits your saliva from doing its job in the digestive process. Are you willing to sacrifice five to ten years of good living in exchange for a quick 5 minutes every now and then?

Faithful practice of the following strategies will remove this challenge from your list of worries. You should:

- Make a conscientious effort to chew your food slowly, carefully, and thoroughly
- Have your teeth examined and cleaned by your dentist at least once per year, but every six months is preferable
- Brush your teeth after each meal and after each time you consume a high-sugar food
- Floss your teeth and/or use your WaterPik every day.

Nutritional Challenge Number Four: As we age, our senses of taste and smell often decline. Smoking and certain medications can, over time, further deteriorate the effectiveness of our taste buds. As important as is the nutritional content of food, the look, taste, and aroma are equally vital. It has been said that we eat first with our eyes. The nose isn't far behind in importance. Further, an old trick, probably recommended by your mother to help you handle bad tasting, malodorous medicine, was to pinch your nose so you couldn't smell it. Somehow that seemed to disguise the bad taste. Though intellectually we can accept that the food on our plate is good for us, if it doesn't look, taste, or smell appealing, we are not likely to eat it. To successfully combat this challenge:

- Drink enough water to guarantee the presence of adequate saliva. Not only is mixing food with saliva the first step in the nutrition extraction process, but saliva also brings out the flavor of the food.
- Take it easy on salt usage. Even if high blood pressure isn't a problem for you, excess salt contributions to dehydration.
- Fight dehydration while adding exciting taste sensations to your dining experiences. Instead of salt, use herbs and spices to heighten the flavor of your food. Even older taste buds thrive when tantalized and motivated by more highly defined food flavors.

Nutritional Challenge Number Five: Along with age and its related declines comes an increase in chronic diseases. Often this is the result of not getting enough antioxidants in your diet. Lurking just below the surface of this important word, antioxidant, is its companion term oxidation, or in simpler terms, rust. In other words, our bodies have a natural tendency to suffer from the human equivalent of rusting. Visualize, if you will, your aging body in the form of an old Desoto automobile, big fins and all that spent its useful life battling the ravages of northern winters. Eventually, car manufactures learned to treat auto bodies with anti-rusting agents with the result that these days, rusting cars have largely disappeared, even from the salt-sprinkled streets of the wintertime north. Your body, too, needs protection from human rust, and that is where antioxidants come in. You can get them just about anywhere in the form of often expensive food supplements. A far better source, however, is from your food—these foods in particular:

- Almonds
- Walnuts
- Bell peppers (especially red and orange)
- Blueberries
- Dark green leafy vegetables
- Strawberries
- Tomatoes
- Beans
- Whole grains
- Just about any brightly colored fruit or vegetable

Nutritional Challenge Number Six: Older adults often suffer from inadequate presence of calcium and vitamin D. Calcium is the main component of our bones. It also helps regulate the nervous system, muscle use, and blood clotting. By far the greatest impact of calcium deficiency is osteoporosis, a deterioration of bone strength. Because of the frequency of osteoporosis, aging adults are at high risk for broken bones, even from the gentlest of falls. The body cannot properly process calcium without vitamin D. Since sunlight and fortified dairy products are the main sources of vitamin D, a supplement may be necessary, particularly if you live in climates with limited sunlight, or if due to diet preferences you don't eat dairy products. Key considerations for calcium intake include:

- The calcium found in dairy foods is especially easy for the body to absorb.
- Make sure any calcium supplements you take contain calcium carbonate or calcium citrate.
- Older adults may need two to three times the currently recommended amounts of vitamin D.
- Other food sources of calcium include:

    1. Leafy green vegetables and yes, former President Bush Senior, that includes broccoli
    2. Certain fruits, especially oranges

3. Beans and peas
4. Fish
5. Sesame seeds

Nutritional Challenge Number Seven: While food is certainly a better source of nutrition than dietary supplements, you will be bombarded with supplement promotions. The following points should help you wade through the swamp of advertisements.

- A multivitamin and a mineral supplement is often all you need.
- Vitamin D and sometimes calcium may be necessary to supplement a healthy diet and preserve bone strength.
- Current research doesn't indicate that antioxidant supplements are essential if you follow a healthy and balanced diet.
- Regardless of what I or anybody else might advise, check with your doctor, or better yet, a nutritionist.

Nutritional Challenge Number Eight: As we age, the sensation of thirst, like so many sensations, decreases. The older we get, the less we seem to notice that we are thirsty. Healthy adults need on average sixty-four ounces of water every day and more when exercising. The fact is, very few body parts function properly when fluid intake is too low. Everything from headaches to fatigue magnify in impact when we don't drink enough fluids. It's so easy to find water but so hard to remember to drink. Caffeine consumption in excess of four to five cups per day can increase urine flow enough to trigger dehydration issues unless sufficient water is consumed to replace the extra urine flow. Excess alcohol intake causes similar problems. You can combat this challenge by:

- Carrying a water bottle with you at all times
- Limiting alcohol consumption

EMPOWERED POSSIBILITIES

- Drinking fluids, such as decaffeinated beverages like water, fruit juices, and/or nonfat/low fat milk
- Remembering to drink extra water when more than five cups of a caffeinated beverage or two or three alcoholic drinks are consumed

In some of the stories shared, you already have a basic idea of how we at Waterman Communities have structured our facilities and programs to empower maximum physical fitness. In the hopes that what we have done will give you some further ideas, however, let me be more specific.

The heart and soul of our fitness program are Holly and Christine, our two well-trained, dedicated, degreed, and enthusiastic fitness professionals. Not only do they supervise our gym and run our wide variety of fitness programs, but both are also available to help our residents and staff members customize their own, unique exercise programs.

In addition, our fully staffed therapy program and our magic fingered massage therapist are available for strength building, injury recovery, and flexibility improvement.

If golfing is your thing, we offer four choices. You can play as often as you like, for only the cost of cart rental at the Mount Dora Golf Association, using our corporate membership. For sharpening your putting skills, use our nine-hole putting green. If you like golf but the Florida heat deters you, play indoors using our golf simulator. In fact, in the simulator you can play some of the world's most famous golf courses. Your fourth option is to use our Wii station. The Wii station, by the way, can be used for bowling or just about any other action game you can think of.

Our out-of-doors facilities include a putting green, a lawn bowling court, a nature trail, shuffleboard, and horseshoes.

EMPOWERED POSSIBILITIES

When it comes to nutrition, our culinary department with its five dining venues simply can't be beat. Virtually every type of food is offered, and our staff dietitian not only assures that each meal is packed with nutrition, but is also available by appointment for individual counseling.

While I hope that this brief review of our fitness-enhancing facilities has been useful to you, most fervently of all I hope that somehow this chapter has inspired you, if you have not done so already, to begin your own fitness program.

If it has, I highly recommend that you first consult your doctor if there is any reason at all to be concerned about your health and your capacity for exercise. Then, with the approval of your physician, find a convenient gym and take a tour. Make sure that it has the machines and classes you want. Since clearly, a result of your exercise program will be your emergence as a stud or a babe (depending on your sex), you'll want to be sure you can be comfortable in the center's prevalent atmosphere. I also recommend that you engage the services of a personal trainer, at least in the beginning. An experienced trainer will help you assess your current condition and get you started on your new fitness program at a level that is best for you.

Just in case you are still hesitating to exercise because of physical limitation, consider the story of my brother-in-law Richard. Several years ago Richard's physician informed him that he suffered from Chronic Obstructive Pulmonary Disease (COPD), a breathing ailment often associated with smoking, and would have to spend the rest of his life tethered to an oxygen tank.

Physically strong and hardened by decades in the construction industry, Richard reveled in being like "Leroy Brown, the Baddest Man" in his town and proud of it. For most of his life, Richard defined the essence of himself as a man by his physical prowess. Quite simply, he could lift more and fight better than most

EMPOWERED POSSIBILITIES

people he met. Now, facing life as an invalid, his normally robust self-confidence crumbled to depression, helplessness, and uncertainty. Fortunately however, it wouldn't last. Though he did grow to appreciate the convenience of the close to the door parking his handicapped sticker brought him, the rest of what it meant to be an invalid was, put simply, unacceptable to him.

One day he showed up at my office, portable oxygen generator and all, looking for some remodeling work. So began the return of "the baddest man in town." At first he wore his oxygen tank. He did present a colorful sight roaring down the road on his antique motorcycle, oxygen line flying in the wind where long hair once had. Later, as his strength increased, the oxygen tank stayed outside in his truck, available for increasingly fewer quick energy blasts.

Today, Richard is staring his sixty-eighth birthday squarely in the face. He works with his hammers, screwdrivers, and saws four ten hour days per week for pay, then helps family members out with odd jobs around their various houses the other three days. His pace is steady and if he ever gets tired, it doesn't show. And the oxygen tanks? He leaves them home now using them only when he sleeps.

How did he do it? He just decided one day that if his disease was going to kill him, he'd rather it did so with a hammer in his hand, so he went back to work and doesn't have any definite plans to stop again. You won't see Richard on the streets jogging anytime soon, and climbing hills isn't his favorite thing to do—unless it's for a good picture he can't get any other way, such as that must have shot of the Golden Gate Bridge he captured last April. But you can see him at work, full-time, passionately doing what he loves and is also quite good at. Admittedly, he paces himself and has finally learned to take breaks. Richard overcame aging and the reality of a life threatening disease just to put a hammer back in his work-toughened hands. What obstacles stand in your way?

EMPOWERED POSSIBILITIES

I hope you'll find the following chart useful as you consider your next steps towards maximum physical fitness.

MY PHYSICAL FITNESS IMPROVEMENT PLAN	
DATE	PHYSICAL FITNESS IMPROVEMENT TACTICS
	Identify an exercise program you can do and enjoy. If necessary, clear it with your physician before starting.
	Find a personal trainer and a gym you are comfortable with.
	Walk rather than drive whenever possible.
	Develop a sound nutrition plan and start following it.
	Identify the foods you enjoy that are high in fat, sugar and/or calorie count and eliminate or at least to limit them in your diet.
	Make sure you drink enough water.
	Focus on improving your balance.
	Maintain muscle flexibility through warm-up and stretching exercise.
	Schedule regular restoration breaks and vacations.

CHAPTER 6:
EMOTIONAL WELLNESS:
OPTIMIZE YOUR OPPORTUNITIES WITH ATTITUDES OF RESILIENCE AND POSSIBILITY

> *Optimism:*
>
> 1. *a tendency to expect the best: the tendency to believe, expect, or hope that things will turn out well*
>
> 2. *confidence: the attitude of somebody who feels positive*
>
> 3. *the doctrine that our world is the best: first proposed by Leibnitz, that ours is the best of all possible worlds*
>
> 4. *a belief in the power of good: philosophy the belief that things are continually getting better and that good will ultimately triumph over evil*

If I were to tell you that you could add both quality and quantity to your life simply by adjusting your attitude, would you be interested? Well, as it happens, that is what I'm telling you. There is solid research that proves that people with a positive attitude live as much as eight to ten years longer than do negative people.

Most of us have grown up with the illustration of the half empty or half full glass. In this illustration, the glass has liquid in it. The perennial question, as you look at the glass: is it half-empty or half-full? How you answer that question reveals a lot about you as a person and your outlook on life.

EMPOWERED POSSIBILITIES

If you see the glass as half-empty, the implication is that your life focus is on what you don't have. It suggests that your perspective centers on what you've lost to the total exclusion of what you still have left. This is the classic position of the pessimist, and it is a life shortening proposition.

If your glass is half-full, your focus very likely emphasizes what you have left and the excitement and satisfaction it can bring into your life. This view suggests a perception that even though there may have been losses in your life, you still have quite a lot of good things left. This is the classic perception of the optimist who always believes that no matter what the present looks like, there are good things coming just around the bend. This, it seems, is a life extending and life-enhancing viewpoint.

Either way you look at it, the glass contains liquid to half its capacity. The perspective of focus and perception provides the key difference. It is, therefore, much better to get what you can from what you have left than to waste your time lamenting what is already gone.

> *Emotional Wellness: Optimize your attitude so you can maximize your opportunities. Maintain a determined, optimistic focus on what you have. Stop worrying about what you don't have.*

Attitudes of optimism with a focus on life's possibilities come in many different shapes, with some having a much more powerful influence on your life than others. But all contribute positively to a longer, better life.

My major goal for this chapter is to convince all readers of the value of being a resilient possibility thinker. Problems and challenges are an inescapable part of life. But in every problem and challenge there truly does live an opportunity, an opportunity that can easily be overlooked if the focus of the individual is on the problem and not on the opportunities it might embody.

EMPOWERED POSSIBILITIES

Just this morning at one of my family's favorite breakfast places, I overheard the following conversation between a server and a departing female customer who was, I estimated, in the neighborhood of seventy-five years old.

"Have a great day!!" said the server.

"Oh, I will," replied the customer, "that's how I choose to live."

Then she continued, "Oh, I may spend five minutes venting to get it out of my system, and then I tell myself, enough!! Let's focus this energy on solving the problem."

I like that approach. Don't you?

Uncle Leslie was the youngest of my father's four brothers. At around the age of twelve, I realized that Uncle Leslie had a character trait that I very much admired. I'll call it persistent resilience. Each time I saw him it seemed that he was involved in a new business venture that often produced much less than he hoped for. He showed his persistent resilience, however, by not letting temporary setbacks become permanent failure. If one plan didn't work out, he hatched a new one, and eventually hit upon tree surgery and apricot growing in western Colorado where he enjoyed success. Persistent resilience is what I admired most about him, and it is the one trait he had that I have most tried to emulate in my life.

Sadly, there was a more than thirty-year gap in our relationship where I only saw him a couple of times. As a young boy I was somewhat in awe of this large, friendly, highly protective and physically capable man. When we reconnected, he was old, bent from the heartbreak of burying two sons, his brush with a sideswiping pickup truck that knocked him down a mountainside, and a heart that had never been quite as strong as his will.

EMPOWERED POSSIBILITIES

Yet even in his weakened condition Uncle Leslie had a remarkable zest for life. He loved to visit his old haunts, out-of-the-way monuments, winding mountain roads, and maybe even an old gold mine or two. Consequently, we traveled a bit on each of my visits, and I got to see parts of Colorado most tourists never do.

He loved to eat out. I can still see the light in his eye and smiling excitement as we sat in a restaurant waiting for him to decide what to order. In many ways I'm sorry to say that I knew Uncle Leslie much better as an old man than I ever did when he was young. But even as an old man, his lifelong practice of persistent resilience wouldn't let any adversity stop him. Oh yes, adversity could slow him down, but stop him? Never!

The following chart contains several attitude words. Positive attitudes are listed on the left and negative attitudes on the right. Please note that each line represents an attitude continuum starting with positive and declining in the direction of negative. In the center is a number grid. Please decide which number best represents where your attitude falls on the attitude continuum and enter that number in the appropriate box on the continuum grid. The positive attitudes listed in the table were chosen because in my research they emerged as key life enhancing attitudes.

When you have completed the exercise, grab a calculator and total your attitude score. The maximum possible score is 200 points. I suspect that anyone completing this exercise with a score above 180 is at least mildly delusional and certainly lacking in honest self-awareness. Beyond that statement, however, I'll leave it up to each individual to determine how satisfactory his/her score is.

> *I couldn't wait for success, so I went ahead without it.*
>
> **Jonathon Winters**

EMPOWERED POSSIBILITIES

KEY ATTITUDES THAT DETERMINE YOUR QUALITY OF LIFE

POSITIVE ATTITUDES	10	9	8	7	6	5	4	3	2	1	NEGATIVE ATTITUDES
Optimism											Pessimism
Unselfish											Selfish
Calm											Anger
Commending											Blaming
Praise											Criticism
Admiration											Cynicism
Trust											Distrust
Gratitude											Entitlement
Generosity											Greed
Love											Hatred
Empathy											Indifference
Tolerant											Intolerant
Supportive											Jealous
Impartial											Prejudiced
Humble											Prideful
Happy for Others											Resentful of others
Forgiving											Revengeful
Trusting											Suspicious
Believing											Skeptical
Thoughtfulness											Thoughtlessness

EMPOWERED POSSIBILITIES

You have no way of answering my questions, as this is not an interactive book, but if you did, I would want to know what you thought about the way you completed the previous exercise in identifying your attitude spectrum. I hope, at least, that you've drawn some conclusions for yourself.

To preserve consistency with our wellness model, I should point out that optimism is an essential ingredient for emotional wellness. What is emotional wellness, other than a reflection of your attitude?

Some years ago, on an employee survey, I read a comment—a call for help, really—that has stayed with me. The comment went like this: "I just wish someone would give me a little praise once in a while." That comment set me to thinking. Was there a way to teach someone what to do in order to earn some praise? Since I love words, I decided to see if I could find a way to use the word praise as an acronym to teach people how to earn praise for themselves. What follows is what I've come up with. I can be so profound sometimes.

Not everyone is a natural optimist. Yet everyone can benefit from taking a more positive outlook on life. To help you do that, I'd like to share with you some suggestions as to how you can take control of your attitude. I've organized these thoughts around the acronym P.R.A.I.S.E. If you incorporate these suggestions into the way you live your life, you will in fact be worthy of praise. I can hear your envious awwws even now. What a brain I have!!

The **P** of praise stands for proprietary thinking. Proprietary thinking means simply "thinking like an owner". In the context of customer service, it is advantageous to employ individuals who think like owners. In this context, a book suggesting ways to empower your ability to live your best life, the P suggests the importance of taking ownership for your life. Very early in this book, I expressed the position that life really is a series of results from the choices each

EMPOWERED POSSIBILITIES

individual has made. Since it is your life and your choices, how could you possibly not take ownership of it?

We live in a world often fixated on finding someone or something to blame for our problems. Before you can truly live your best life, before you can take control and make good things happen, you first have to take ownership of whatever situation you are in. That situation, be it good or bad, happened because of choices you made. So take ownership. Not only will ownership give you a better understanding and perspective on the events of your past, but it will also prepare you to more effectively deal with your future. Ownership is a key element of optimism.

> **The Myth:** *It's best to expect the worst. That way you are always ready, and you are never surprised.* **The Facts:** *Focusing on the negative shortens your life, lowers your satisfaction, and makes you unpleasant to be around.*

Now I hope you have noticed by this time that with the **P** gone from the word praise, you are left with another word, raise. R.A.I.S.E., too, is an acronym that describes how thinking like the owner of your life will look. As the proprietor, owning your life raises your self-esteem, increases the respect that others feel for you, and ultimately earns you praise both from yourself and others. Yes, I meant it in the previous sentence when I said ownership of your life will earn you praise from yourself. As difficult as some of our self-constructed realities are to face and accept, there is ultimately a great sense of power and control when we do. Therefore we can say, take proprietary ownership of your life and R.A.I.S.E. your satisfaction level significantly. Let's move on to see how it's done.

The **R** stands for "respect the individual". Since you are the individual in question here, it is important that you begin with a healthy and balanced self-respect. With an attitude of proper self-respect, you will naturally want to take care of yourself. You will want to exercise, eat right, and feed your mind the solid food of continuous learning. It is much easier to feel positive about life when you feel healthy, mentally sharp, and capable.

The **A** stands for "anticipate your own future". Early into my research in this topic I found the following brief statement on a website I was visiting: "Everyone needs someone to love, something to do, and something to look forward to."

> *Focusing on the good in life leads to greater satisfaction with and appreciation for the better and the best things. In the process, the bad things seem either not to happen or even if they do, not to amount to much.*

In that one statement, by the way, I found the seeds for three of my seven principles for successful aging and living your best life. In my first principle, engaging in meaningful activities, I covered the part about having something to do. In my last principle, relationships, we'll talk about the importance of having someone to love. For purposes of this discussion right now however, we'll focus on the importance of having something to look forward to.

Anticipating your future means planning for it. It means having future goals that are worth looking forward to—that in fact, make your life worth getting up in the morning for and living. Someone reminded me recently that it also involves following a financial plan designed to assure your ability to afford your target lifestyle. A major, positive impact on your level of optimism lies in whether your future holds exciting things you are looking forward to and can afford to pursue. Make sure that it does.

We've all heard the joke about the senior citizen overheard remarking, "I'm so old and my life is so uncertain that I don't even buy green bananas. Long-range planning for me is pretty much limited to what to have for lunch."

EMPOWERED POSSIBILITIES

That statement does not reflect optimism. No possibility thinking is taking place there. There is not even a hint of potential for resilience in overcoming challenge. In fact, it's a quite pessimistic expression suggesting the rapidly emerging reality of death, which may or may not be true. One thing is certain, however: so powerful are our thoughts, they often make themselves come true. Our attitudes exercise so much control over us that the seemingly simple act of nurturing negative thoughts increases the risk that the things we most fear and worry about will happen. The mind is, therefore, both a wonderful and terrible thing, depending on how you let it spend its time.

If you would truly like to live your life as an optimistic, resilient possibility thinker, make sure that you put something into each day of your future that you can look forward to. It doesn't matter what it is. It only has to have meaning for you. But it does have to be there.

The letter I represents the need to initiate action, and then take steps to insure the desired results. Have you ever found yourself wondering why an old friend hasn't called in a while? Did your thoughts go something like this: "I don't know what's wrong with Sally. I haven't heard from her in months"?

If you felt that way about a friend, has it ever occurred to you to carry the thought a logical step further, by asking yourself, "How long has it been since Sally last heard from me?"

Do you see the point? It might be true that I haven't heard from Sally in quite a while. It is just as possible that Sally has not heard from me in quite a while either. Just as I am wondering what has happened to her, she might also be wondering what has happened to me. Soon both Sally and I are circling in a fruitless holding pattern waiting for the other to initiate contact.

> *Growing older is mandatory; acting older is optional.*

EMPOWERED POSSIBILITIES

In situations like the above, the optimist doesn't wait to be contacted, all the while worrying that something might have gone wrong. The optimist initiates contact and as a result seldom finds anything wrong. What is there about the human animal that so often sidelines us while waiting for someone else to initiate action and/or contact?

> You are not obligated to win. You're obligated to keep trying to do the best you can, every day.
>
> Marian Wright Edelman

If you aren't satisfied with the way your life is going, if it seems there are more negative things headed your way than there are positive things, do something about it. Take ownership of your situation and initiate positive action.

If your problem is loneliness and it seems you don't have any friends, initiate contact. As nice as you might be, unless you're a celebrity, or otherwise magnetically desirable, you shouldn't expect to see, just around the next corner, a crowd of people jostling to be first to offer you friendship. It is far more likely that if there is a crowd of people around the next corner, many of them are as lonely as you are. In fact, why don't you stop reading right now and take a quick glance around you. Unless you are completely alone, there's a very good chance that your next new friend is sitting or standing only a few steps away. One of you needs to initiate contact or the friendship will never be.

> Let me tell you the secret that has led me to my goal. My strength lies solely in my tenacity.
>
> Louis Pasteur

As is common to virtually everyone I've met, my life is well-sprinkled with periods of great challenge, most of which, upon reflection, were and continue to be self-generated.

EMPOWERED POSSIBILITIES

I remember a time nearly twenty years ago when my transition from employee to independent consultant wasn't going as planned. I was running low on money, and saw few prospects. With two young children, a wife, a dog, an elderly aunt, and several concerned creditors depending on me for support, I was worried. Normally an optimist by nature, I allowed the uncertainties of self-employment to overpower nearly every other aspect of my life. Soon, I encaged myself in mind numbing, action freezing depression. Things got so bad that I actually envisioned myself and my family living, homeless, under an overpass of the Brooklyn Queens Expressway in New York City. I hadn't liked that highway when I lived near it, and now it occupied a prominent place in my nightmares. The certainty of my looming failure was all I could think about.

Fortunately our caring family doctor helped me break a very dangerous pattern. I didn't fail; nor did I run out of money. In fact, my consulting business thrived for several pretty good years.

> *We are shaped by our thoughts. We become what we think.*
>
> **Buddha**

From those times I learned a very valuable lesson. I own my life. I have a God I can call on and a family that supports me, including a brother and sister-in-law who stood ready to take us in, but it's still my life as lived through my choices. Only I could confront my challenges and make something happen. Sure, I might confront my fears and demons backed up by God and family, but deliverance still requires action from me.

In my case, the path out of that jungle of my own making started with a phone call to a colleague who as it turned out, had been thinking about calling me to discuss some work he wanted done. His name was Glen Choban and I don't believe he knows yet, to this day, the key role he played in saving me from the prison of despair I had built for myself. Thanks Glen, just in case I didn't tell you before.

The point is, as challenged and as low as I felt, I made myself initiate action. No matter what the challenge, initiating some kind of action, even if it's small, always makes me feel better, more positive, about my future. Try it yourself; you might like it.

The letter **I** also means "insure the solution". Sometimes one call doesn't net you the business. Knocking on the door of your closest neighbor may not initiate the friendship you're looking for. It often takes several calls and several doors knocked on. Most of all, it means never give up, and that requires persistence. Persistence is the insurance you often must buy in order to guarantee success.

Some years ago, it was my privilege to serve on a college advisory board with an energetic gentleman who owned more than two hundred nursing homes. He was an inspiration to be with, and as you can imagine, a regular topic of discussion among those who knew him, particularly when he wasn't around. What made him special, so successful, we all wondered?

In a private conversation with his corporate pilot I learned the following:

"When I first came to work for him, I expected to find someone of well-above-average intelligence. However, after getting to know him, I decided that he might not even be intellectually as smart as me. Yet he was certainly more successful. Ultimately, the only conclusion I could draw was that when others gave up, he kept moving forward. It wasn't that he was so smart; it's just that he was so persistently sure of his goals that he never gave up. In most deals, he very simply was the last man standing."

EMPOWERED POSSIBILITIES

Sable diligently continues her pursuit of the relentlessly, reluctant, and illusive glow.

That's an excellent example of the power of persistence. It isn't enough just to initiate action. You must also insure its success with positively applied persistence.

My dog, Sable, is the epitome of persistent optimism. Well into her twelfth year of life— senior citizenship status for a boxer—Sable keeps herself in good shape. She doesn't overeat. She exercises regularly as is testified by the broad collection of throwing and tossing toys scattered about our house. She gets plenty of sleep, and as far as I can see there is little stress in her life except for those occasions when she wants to play and I don't. In short, though old for a dog, she is quite alert and well oriented. Well oriented, that is, except for one small detail.

If we take our showers at just the right time in the morning with the sun shining strategically through our tall bathroom window, its reflection catches the opening and closing of the shower door, casting an oddly shaped and moving glow on the wall and the sink. Sable has fervently chased that glow for almost twelve years. I know she has no hope of catching it, but she doesn't. Consequently, she never gives up. She believes in her little doggie heart that one day she will catch that reflection.

She's very serious about it. Occasionally, if the glow stays still for longer than a few seconds she will actually bite that spot on the door or wall. By the way, even after twelve futile years of trying, she doesn't seem the least bit discouraged. Wouldn't it be nice

EMPOWERED POSSIBILITIES

if we, human beings reputed to be of much higher intelligence than dogs, stopped giving up on our goals because we believe they're impossible, and kept persisting?

The **S** stands for "surpass expectations". This principle has a two-way focus. First, surpass or go farther in a positive direction then even you might think possible. Second, in all your dealings with others, surpass their expectations too. Some years back, an insurance agent friend of mine promoted among his staff the concept of doing just one more thing to earn customer satisfaction. His watchword became, do just one more thing. Simple, yes, yet it was very effective in helping him and his agency achieve and actually surpass their goals.

> Even if you win the rat race, you are still a rat.

Determining to surpass the minimum expected in every situation is an important companion to the attitude of persistence described above. Persisting and determining to give more than expected do wonders for the attitudes of those around you and pay double dividends on your own attitude.

The **E** stands for "engage". A quote from the Bible comes to mind. It goes something like this: "If a man wishes to have friends, he must show himself friendly." One of the best things you can do for your attitude is to engage, participate, and get involved in what is going on around you. In this, I am simply repeating, in short form, the admonitions of chapter 4.

The reality is, not everyone is an optimist. Furthermore, it is possible that for a brief time at least, even an optimist can feel pessimistic. I, quite accidentally, stumbled upon a simple and certain method for giving even an abject pessimist a quick, pleasant, and often lasting booster shot of optimism. In fact, this technique is so simple you might not even think it's worth trying. But here it is

EMPOWERED POSSIBILITIES

anyway: smile. That's it, smile. Yes, it really is that simple. And the really good news is that it's oh so effective.

To prove me right, why don't you join me in a simple experiment? Here we go. Think about something that always makes you happy. In my case, it's my two grandchildren Riley and Reed. I can't think of them without smiling. As I smile I can literally feel my attitude improve and my stress dissolve.

> *Laughing is good exercise. It's like jogging on the inside, and it can be done without sweating.*

I'm sure that as you just now allowed a happy thought to cross your mind, you simply had to smile. Close your eyes if you have to, but try to relive the feeling that embraced you when you thought that happy thought. Didn't your mood elevate? Couldn't you literally feel the stress dissolving around you? How could you help it?

I think I can safely say that no one can think a happy thought without smiling. And further, no one can smile without elevating their mood, even if only briefly. There are more benefits to a smile, however, than a brief elevation of spirit.

If you walk down the streets of your life with a smile on your face, the people you meet will, quite naturally, think well of you. With a smile on your face, you will project an air of confidence that you might not actually feel. At the very least, your smile will stoke the curiosity of those you meet. They'll drive themselves crazy trying to identify what you know that they don't. People who smile around the workplace have been proven to get more promotions. They are easier to approach. Very simply, with a smile on your face at meetings and appointments, the people you are with will react much more positively to you.

EMPOWERED POSSIBILITIES

Just to bring home my point with stronger emphasis, I present to you the following list of benefits associated with a smile. Smiling will:

- Make you more attractive
- Change your mood
- Spread optimism with the speed of lightning
- Boost your immune system
- Lower your blood pressure
- Release endorphins, (natural painkillers), and serotonin
- Lift your face, make you look younger, and if only briefly, spare you the expense of plastic surgery
- Help you stay positive even in the face of challenge and we've already proven that to be good for your health

A very attractive woman works out at the gym the same time I do. Of the thirty or forty people working out at that time, few if any are more focused on exercise than is she. In fact, she is so serious about her exercise and so focused on hitting her repetition goals that she barely seems to notice the rest of us. She will respond to a greeting but if you want to talk to her, it must be when she is on a machine, because she doesn't and won't stop. Consequently, she seldom smiles and is often thought of as unapproachable, disinterested in others, and unfriendly. Yet when you amass the courage to approach her, the smile you receive is transformational. She goes from merely attractive to beautiful and you find a bright, pleasant, and engaging conversationalist. I wish she would smile more. She could easily smile and continue to concentrate on her exercise routines.

She sometimes complains of being lonely, and that has to be because of her aura of inapproachability. Few people I know have

Balance endless possibilities with realistic expectations, keeping in mind that the fun is in the journey, not in the destination.

EMPOWERED POSSIBILITIES

less reason to be alone. She doesn't want to spend so much time alone and she really is easy to approach once you know her. Replacing the frown of concentration with a smile of determined warmth is the key. If she smiled more she would be happier and could still maintain peak physical condition.

So what do you think? If you're a pessimist, are you ready to start living your life as an optimist? As is true with most new skills, to a certain extent you can train yourself in the skill of optimism. The more naturally pessimistic you are and the longer you have lived from that life perspective, the more difficult it will be; but with effort, determination, and a smile, you can succeed.

Some of the benefits of a positive attitude include:

- A longer life by as much as eight to ten years
- Better health
- More energy
- Higher level of immunity to disease
- Increased tolerance of pain
- More successful relationships
- Superior work performance, bringing with it higher pay, a greater sense of fulfillment, and more promotions
- Better decision making
- More likely to be perceived as a leader

One of the most vital aspects of an optimistic spirit is gratitude. Being thankful has long been established as a key characteristic of those who live and age successfully. If your life is so filled with turmoil, challenge and trouble that you seldom feel thankful, try this. Start a thankfulness notebook. In it at the end of each day, write down at least five good things that happened to you that day for which you are thankful. Do that every day, being sure to review your list regularly. You'll be surprised how soon and how dramatically your attitude will change for the better.

EMPOWERED POSSIBILITIES

I've said it before, but I'll say it again. Life is full of challenges that, if we aren't careful, easily become progress-blocking obstacles. I introduced the topic of resilience with a brief description of my Uncle Leslie. Nothing ever kept him down for very long—business reversals, the deaths of two sons, a semi-invalid wife, being hit by a truck as he bent under the hood of his own truck, and chronic heart disease—none of those things kept him down. A quick recovery from setback is the essence of a resilient spirit. Resilience is the cornerstone of a positive attitude.

Tucked securely within the definition of resilience is the concept of elasticity, defined by my dictionary as the ability of matter to spring back quickly into shape after being bent, stretched, or deformed.

Sometimes life comes at us in ways that bend, stretch, and even deform us. It is in those most challenging of times that we need to be most resilient, and that requires flexibility, buoyancy, an unconquerable spirit, and gentle toughness. My friend Sam shared this story about his first experience with a hurricane:

Sam, for many years, resisted leaving the wintery cold of Massachusetts for the warmth of sunny Florida for one main reason. He wanted nothing to do with hurricanes. Finally he surrendered to the lure and promises of year round warmth and moved. He made his move the same year that Central Florida survived three hurricanes.

Standing in his living room in front of his large picture window, his wife, dogs, and daughter safely tucked away in the laundry room, Sam settled in to watch his first hurricane. Two types of trees occupied his yard: slender, graceful palms and the mighty oaks of poetic fame. As Sam watched the relentless attacks of Hurricane Charlie, the palms bent almost horizontal to the ground. The Oaks, on the other hand, refused to bend, standing tall, hardy, tough, and resistance in the face of Charlie's

EMPOWERED POSSIBILITIES

relentless and powerful pummeling. At the end of the storm, all of Sam's Palms simply stood up still rooted firmly in the ground. His largest Oak lay on its side, powerful and stubborn but its subdued roots exposed to the sky.

The oak, powerful, sturdy, hardy, and tough as it was, failed the test of resilience. The palms, too, proved powerful, sturdy, hardy, and tough but in addition, they were flexible and elastic in their resilient toughness. They could bounce back, but the stubborn, inflexible Oak could only uproot and fall.

You cannot be resilient if you aren't hardy and tough, but you must also be flexible and optimistic. The Oak is a much prettier tree and far statelier in the good times, but it is the resilient palm tree that faces and survives the big storms.

If I haven't already convinced you of the benefits of becoming an optimist, if you aren't one already, let me share with you some of the things we've built in to our internal environment in our Waterman Communities that are designed to foster optimism. I hope they give you some ideas.

First and foremost, we have made negative attitudes a performance issue. If it is true that a positive attitude can lengthen your life, then it follows that a negative attitude will shorten your life. Furthermore, just as a smile will spread positive attitudes, a frown will spread negative attitudes. In fact, the truth seems to be that a negative attitude will spread much further and more effectively than a positive one. In the service industry, we have known for a while that a customer who enjoys a good service experience may tell two or three people, but the individual who endures a bad service experience is quite likely to tell eleven. All you have to do is watch the evening news on television to realize that negative news sells much more effectively than positive news.

EMPOWERED POSSIBILITIES

Consequently, we will discipline the constant, non-constructive complainers. Our point is to get rid of the problem behavior, and we hope that in the process we get to keep the individual. But if the individual absolutely will not give up the negative behavior, we will have no choice but to eliminate the behavior by bidding farewell to the individual. If that sounds harsh to you, consider this: would you tolerate the presence of a cancer in your body simply because it was a part of you? I don't think so! Neither then, should you tolerate indefinitely the presence of a negative person, for their negativity is a cancer every bit as damaging to the life of your organization and your own personal well-being as is a cancerous disease running rampant in your body. Just as a cancer consumes the healthy cells around it until your body is destroyed, negativity saps the energy of everyone forced to endure it—and that includes the negative people themselves.

Communication plays a key role in affecting people's attitudes. With this thought in mind, we are ever increasing our use of our in-house TV station as an effective communication tool. Most recently, we began a weekly newscast during which I answer all the questions that have been brought to my attention in the previous week. I will even answer the questions I would rather not answer. In fact, the only questions I won't answer are those that would embarrass specific individuals. By the way, though I don't necessarily enjoy it, I will answer questions designed to embarrass me.

I hope that if you are already an optimist, you will continue happily to be one. And if you have been to this point a pessimist, consider changing. If pessimism is a cancer, then it is deadly. If it is deadly, it will eventually kill you and the innocents forced to be around you. Even though it may

> **Your sense of humor is one of the most powerful tools you have to make certain that your daily mood and emotional state support good health.**
>
> Paul E. McGhee, PhD

EMPOWERED POSSIBILITIES

be a scientifically proven fact that pessimists don't live as long as optimists, to those living with the pessimist, life can be a seemingly long and tortured experience. Wouldn't it be better to actually live a long life than to live a shorter, negative life that feels like a very, very long life to those living it with you? Think about it.

One of the easiest ways to deflect pessimism is to laugh. Laughter brings about healthy physical changes in the body. Humor and laughter strengthen your immune system. They can also up your energy, diminish aches and pains, and help to protect you from the damaging effects of stress. The best part is that this priceless medicine is fun, free, and readily available.

A good ole belly laugh relieves physical tension and stress, leaving your muscles relaxed for up to forty-five minutes afterward. By laughing you will decrease stress hormones and increase immune cells and infection-fighting antibodies, thus improving your resistance to disease. Laughter also triggers the release of endorphins, the body's natural feel-good chemicals. Endorphins promote an overall sense of well-being and can even temporarily relieve pain. Laughter improves the function of blood vessels and increases blood flow, which in turn can help protect you against a heart attack and other cardiovascular problems.

The many benefits of laughter not only include physical but also mental health benefits. Some of these are:

- Added joy and zest to life
- Less anxiety and fear
- Less stress
- Better mood
- Enhanced resilience

There is a direct link between laughter and mental health. Laughter melts distressing emotions away. You can't feel anxious, angry, or sad when you're laughing!

EMPOWERED POSSIBILITIES

Laughter helps you relax and recharge. It increases energy, helping you to stay focused and accomplish more. Humor can shift your perspective, allowing you to see situations in a more realistic, less threatening light. A humorous perspective creates psychological distance, which can help you avoid feeling overwhelmed.

Before proceeding to the next chapter, take a few moments to review the following table. In it you will find a listing of several of the attitude-improving tactics discussed in this chapter. Consider each tactic carefully, and then in the space to the left of each attitude improvement statement, enter a projected date by which you plan to implement that tactic in your life.

MY ATTITUDE IMPROVEMENT PLAN	
DATE	ATTITUDE IMPROVEMENT TACTICS
	Focus on possibilities rather than impossibilities. Don't let the obstacles keep you from discovering the opportunities.
	Keep a running list of the things you are thankful for.
	Limit your contact with negative people.
	Surround yourself with positive, upbeat yet realistic people.
	Stop worrying about the things you cannot do and focus instead on the things you can.
	Look for reasons to praise and commend rather than criticize.
	Keep a smile on your face.
	Develop a formal plan for securing your financial future.
	Make a list of future plans you are looking forward to.
	Move your focus from your problems and challenges to your solutions and opportunities.

MY ATTITUDE IMPROVEMENT PLAN	
DATE	ATTITUDE IMPROVEMENT TACTICS
	In every task or project do at least one more thing than necessary.
	Practice being happy for the blessings that come to others and thankful for the ones that come to you.
	Keep your antennae always out and search for the many good things that are happening even while bad things are happening.

CHAPTER 7:
SPIRITUAL WELLNESS:
WORSHIP AND WIELD THE ENERGY AND STRENGTH THAT COME FROM PUTTING YOUR FAITH IN A HIGHER POWER

Worship:

1. *To treat somebody or something as a deity: to treat somebody or something as divine and show respect by engaging in acts of prayer and devotion*

2. *Take part in a religious service*

3. *Love somebody deeply: to love, admire, or respect somebody or something greatly and perhaps excessively or unquestioningly*

4. *Religious adoration: the adoration, devotion, and respect given to a deity*

5. *Religious rites: the rites or services through which people show their adoration, devotion, and respect for a deity*

6. *Great devotion: great or excessive love, admiration, and respect felt for somebody or something*

The concept of **Spiritual Wellness** has long been recognized as part of the wellness equation. Putting your faith and trust in a higher power outside of the self can lead to better physical and mental health and greater longevity. This higher power of which I speak is commonly thought of as God, even if the specific name is something different like Allah, Jehovah, and even the Great Spirit among the many other names. Virtually every society has, somewhere near

EMPOWERED POSSIBILITIES

its roots, a higher power that is the object of worship, adoration, and sometimes fear, and is the source of strength and inspiration for that society.

For some, it's a collection of higher powers, or gods, each with a role to play, and the roles are not always played in complete harmony. For others, it is a way of life, a system for attaining inner knowledge and peace, usually originated by a leader such as the Buddha. Regardless of its form or focus, faith and worship are powerful elements in the lives of those who practice them.

The benefits of having a God to believe in are fully realized in the face of problems that seem simply too big to handle alone. There is great comfort and security in having a higher power to tap into for assistance. There is wonderful relief that even in the face of impending doom, there is a haven and a sanctuary to flee to.

Recent polls suggest that 95 percent of all residents of the United States believe in God in some form. The importance of spirituality is especially strong in the over sixty-five population. 75 percent of the over sixty-five population say they are members of a church and

> *Spiritual Wellness: Worship and put faith and trust in a higher power outside of yourself.*

as many as 60 percent attend church regularly. Reasons for this increased emphasis on spirituality among older people are likely found in the increased health, safety, and security issues faced by that population. After all, fear, illness, and adversity have long been effective motivators, driving people of all ages to God. He's used to it by the way, though He certainly does appreciate contact in the good times as well.

Unfortunately, medicine, which ironically traces its modern roots to early religious orders, has largely lost its focus on the healing benefits of faith and prayer. For many physicians, science is now the God. Yet it is obvious that many of their patients particularly

EMPOWERED POSSIBILITIES

the older ones—rely on faith and prayer, along with modern medicine and advanced medical skills.

Because I'm a Christian, it's easier for me to approach the subject of faith from the Christian perspective. In so doing, however, I believe the principles described apply to sound spiritual health in any major world religion.

> **The Myth:** Even if there is a God, he couldn't possibly be interested in my meager little affairs. **The Facts:** The older we get, the more we are aware of just how important our God is to us and how much His love sustains us.

Christians are taught that one of the reasons God created mankind was to have something to love that could also love in return. By implication, then say the Christians, not only does God want to be loved, but it is our obligation to worship him, for no other reason than that he deserves it.

I find nothing in this position to dispute as far as it goes. Ours is a good God and certainly deserving of worship. On this point, however, we find one of the myriad differences between God and man. While it is true that God appreciates our worship and even desires it, he doesn't need it. Man, on the other hand, seems actually to need to worship a higher power. Without this critical faith connection, mankind, atheistic protestations aside, never quite attains total peace.

Theologians have wrestled with this issue for centuries. One twentieth century theologian whose name I no longer recall put it this way: "If there was no God, we would have to invent one."

Another theologian, Paul Tillich, said, "God is the symbol of our ultimate concern." You might have to think about that statement for a while, but I promise you, it will eventually make sense to you.

EMPOWERED POSSIBILITIES

Anyway, how often do I, a simple businessman, get to quote, by name, a great theologian?

Theological arguments aside, however, there are distinct health advantages to worshiping a higher power. Research shows that worship of and putting your faith in a higher power brings health benefits roughly equal to exercise and eating right. (Incidentally for you couch potatoes, the operative phrase in the preceding sentence is "roughly equal to.") Going to church does not eliminate the need for regular exercise and proper nutrition. It supplements them.

Why might this be true?

The answer, I think, lies in the content of our worship. A common form of worship is prayer. Unfortunately, many if not most prayers are issued with a strong sense of urgency for protection, relief, release, and/or the granting of requests. This type of connection to a higher power is really only a small part of worship.

In the following spaces, list the characteristics of your God as you understand Him.

1. _____
   _____
2. _____
   _____
3. _____
   _____
4. _____
   _____
5. _____
   _____

What is your personal relationship like with the God you just described?

_____
_____

In what ways might you like to improve that relationship?

_____
_____

EMPOWERED POSSIBILITIES

To help you understand what I mean, let's go back to our discussion on attitude. You will remember that a positive attitude adds quality and quantity to your life. You will further remember that in many respects, the events of our lives reflect what we spend our time focusing on. If your only form of worship contains pleas for help or requests for deliverance, you are missing the most powerful value of worship. You are focusing on your problems and more than likely, you are missing your blessings. In fact, by concentrating your prayers solely on your wants, fears, and needs without adding the benefits of praise and thanksgiving, you could actually be making your problems worse. What are your thoughts?

What are the positive benefits of worship that go beyond having our temporal needs met and our challenges dealt with? What can worship bring into our lives when we expand our focus beyond fear- and/or concern driven requests?

> **Deut 30:15:** "See I have set before you this day life and prosperity, and death and adversity; in that I command you today to love the Lord your God...that the Lord may bless you in the land...but if your heart turns away and you will not obey, but worship other gods...you will surely perish."

True worship, the kind that improves your health and adds both quality and quantity to your years, includes gratitude, thanksgiving, love, adoration, praise, and anticipation of good and exciting things God will do for you in the future. True worship emphasizes and strengthens your trust and along with it, confidence. Because prayer is often a request for guidance, it is quite likely that prayer leads to better decisions. Also, let me add with emphasis, nothing I have said so far should suggest to you that bringing your cares and concerns to your God are a bad thing. I am saying, however, that if that's all you do, you are severely missing out on the major benefits of worship.

EMPOWERED POSSIBILITIES

Prayer increases your sense of commitment. Remember our earlier discussions on the benefits of engagement and of determining to matter and make a difference? Think back to the chapter on attitude and note that all of the aspects of worship I just mentioned are positive attitudes.

Further, prayer enhances your sense of power and control. After all, if my prayer can influence the outcome of the events I'm concerned about, what need is there for me to worry so much? Put simply, true worship, of which prayer is a vital part, is a celebration of positive attitudes revolving around your God. No wonder worship adds quality and quantity to your years.

Keep in mind that nowhere does God promise to spare us from trouble, testing, and challenge. He does, however, promise to limit our exposure to only those adversities we can bear with the help of His strength and support.

> *Religious interventions in religious patients with depression, anxiety, bereavement, and pain caused depressive symptoms, anxiety, and bereavement to become better more quickly. This was not only Christian interventions, but also Buddhist as well as Islamic interventions.*
>
> Dr. Harold G. Koenig

True worship ultimately forces you to think beyond your problems and challenges and to focus on the many good things in your life. It gives you hope. It gives you comfort. It gives you inner peace. And most of all, it reminds you that no problem you might ever face is too big for you and your God to handle. There is energizing, healing power in that belief.

And, for the one-god world religions, Judaism, Christianity, and Islam, there is more. According to the Bible, in the early days after creation, Adam, Eve, and God walked together talking face-to-face every evening in the Garden of Eden. Not only was God an object of Adam and Eve's worship, but also he was their friend.

EMPOWERED POSSIBILITIES

It was this face-to-face, communal relationship that was most damaged as a result of sin. Praising the Lord through worship, communing with Him in prayer, reminding ourselves of how good and great He is, studying His word, and reveling in the magnificence of His creation constitute our only avenues to a relationship with God. In just a couple of chapters, we will be discussing how important positive relationships are to living your best life. Therefore, it seems that it is important to have positive relationships not only with our friends and family, but also with our God.

We should think of the benefits of worship in much the same way we think of the benefits provided to us by our employers. Our employers, through the benefit package they provide, offer protection from all manner of risk, including health, loss of life, and income. We wouldn't think of turning down these benefits unless the cost too great for us to bear. The beautiful thing about the benefits of worship is that they are ours automatically through our faith and at no cost beyond the commitment of our time.

The more we worship, the stronger our faith. As our faith strengthens, our attitudes improve and some even believe that our minds grow stronger. Increased faith leads to increased confidence. Many of our fears dissipate. Our priorities clarify and our mission becomes more focused. These benefits are ours, not only through individual but also collective worship.

Earlier I referenced research that indicates that the health benefits of worship and faith in a higher power are similar to those of exercise and proper nutrition. Specifically, several studies have shown that people who pray are less likely to get sick than people who don't, and when they do get sick they don't get as sick nor are they

> *Stress and depression can cause psychosomatic illness. Psychosomatic illness can lead people to believe that they have physical ailments and this belief causes the symptoms to actually occur.*
>
> *Janis Masyk-Jackson*

EMPOWERED POSSIBILITIES

sick for as long. Blood pressure among people who pray regularly tends to be lower. Further, people who pray seem to have lower rates of depression and suicide. It must be emphasized, however, that the healing power of prayer is most effective when praying is a regular rather than a reactive part of the individual's life.

In 1988, heart surgeon Dr. Randolph C. Byrd published an article in the *Southern Medical Journal* describing a study conducted with 393 coronary heart disease patients whose symptoms were similar. The patients were divided into two groups, with one group being prayed for, while the other was not. None of the participants knew which group they were in. By the end of the study records showed clearly that the patients in the prayed for group required fewer drugs and significantly less ventilation assistance, and showed fewer cases of pneumonia than did those who were not prayed for. To me that is an amazing fact. It is possible that the only prayers that went up on behalf of the individuals in the study were those prayed by others—and those being prayed for didn't even know it. Yet they showed more improvement than did those who were not prayed for, who also didn't know they weren't being prayed for. How do you explain that? The power of prayer on behalf of others is a complete mystery to me, but a mystery I'm pleased to live with.

Let me reference just one more study on this topic before I move on. A 1998 study involving forty AIDS patients and published in the *Western Journal of Medicine* showed that those who were prayed for by total strangers in general felt better and had fewer significant health incidences than those who were not prayed for. There's that beautiful mystery again!

Clearly, prayer can be a significant factor in enhancing the quality and quantity of your life. Fortunately, there does not seem to be either a precisely right or a precisely wrong way to pray. Just as human friendships are nurtured while sitting down, standing up, walking, talking, working, and engaging in physically challenging activities, so it appears can your relationship with your God also be nourished and nurtured from a variety of bodily postures.

When praying, you can kneel if you choose or remain standing. You can close your eyes or leave them open. You can fold your hands and bow your head or continue with the posture you are using at the time you decided to pray. You can use the language of seventeenth-century England as found in the *King James Bible* or the language you communicate in every day. You can think of Him as Your God or Thy God; either way, God will hear, understand, and respond.

"But what," you might be asking, "about meditation?"

The purpose of meditation is to rid the body of negative energy, replacing it with positive energy. In so doing, the mind relaxes, allowing it to focus on those elements of body and spirit where improvement is needed.

The concept and importance of meditation is well documented in Scripture, particularly by the psalmist. I'll share just two examples with you.

> Ps 145:5
> On the glorious splendor of thy majesty, and on thy wondrous works, I will meditate. RSV

> Phil 4:8-9
> Finally, brethren, whatever things are true, whatever things are noble, whatever things are just, whatever things are pure, whatever things are lovely, whatever things are of good report, if there is any virtue and if there is anything praiseworthy—meditate on these things. 9 The things which you learned and received and heard and saw in me, these do, and the God of peace will be with you. NKJV

EMPOWERED POSSIBILITIES

Given the support for meditation in the scriptures, it would seem that meditation combined with prayer could make a powerful impact on lives.

Just as with prayer, the health benefits of meditation include less stress, resulting in lower blood pressure, leading to reduced risk of heart attack. Meditation can also lead to a lessened awareness of pain.

My wife, Janet, lived this truth, with me faithfully at her side, during the births of our two children. We were proud graduates of Lamaze training. By the way, I believe that Lamaze is a form of meditation. It worked. Janet, in normal circumstances, has a very low tolerance for pain. Yet she went through both births without the intervention of pain preventing medication. I do not recall what she focused on for the birth of our daughter, but when our son was born she focused, meditated on, if you will, a picture of our daughter, and it carried her through the pain.

> *How much listening do you do for what God has to say to you?*
>
> _____
> _____
> _____
>
> *What are your thoughts on your answer?*
>
> _____
> _____
> _____

The power of meditation emanates from its ability to generate calm and internal peace, thus enhancing the individual's sense of emotional well-being. And that, as you can see, is very much like prayer. Improved emotional well-being leads to a greater sense of purpose and direction as well as better relationships.

So now you might be asking, "Which is better, prayer or meditation?"

EMPOWERED POSSIBILITIES

For me the answer is both. Prayer is, after all, a form of talking. Often, when we're talking we aren't listening. Since God seldom speaks to us audibly, we often, in our prayers, fail to hear what He has to say. Meditation is all about listening. In fact, we might even find in the Bible an endorsement of meditation from God himself.

Perhaps Psalm 46:10 will help you understand what I mean. It reads in the language of the New Living Translation of the Bible, "Be still, and know that I am God!" How do you like that?!! God is telling us to be still in order to know Him!!

The *Bible Exposition Commentary* adds this thought- "Be still, and know that I am God" (Ps 46:10, KJV). This is a wonderful antidote for a restless spirit. The Hebrew word translated is "be still" means "take your hands off, relax." It's so easy for us to get impatient with the Lord and start meddling in matters that we ought to leave alone. He is God, and His hands can accomplish the impossible. Our hands may get in the way and make matters worse (*The Bible Exposition Commentary: Old Testament* © 2001-2004 by Warren W. Wiersbe. All rights reserved.)

In our worship experience, there is a time to be still so we may listen and hear what God wants to say. There is, in other words, a time and a place for meditation.

There is a body of evidence that clearly suggests that combining prayer with meditation techniques strengthens the effects of both. Try it. You will be unleashing incredible power.

The benefits of spiritual connection are many and varied. Once connected to a higher power through prayer, meditation, thanksgiving, praise, and study, you can expect to enjoy the following benefits:

- As your mind opens more and more to new ideas, insights, and experiences, you will ultimately study and

EMPOWERED POSSIBILITIES

learn from a variety of cultures and religions, thus broadening your world view.
- Your code of ethics will solidify behind higher standards.
- Your decisions will be better and more consistent with your values.
- You will enjoy the peace and security that comes from knowing you can tap in to the resources of a higher power.
- You will profit from closer relationships with the body of like believers.
- You will come to better understand your natural talents, strengths, and weaknesses, and this understanding will lead you down a more satisfying life path.
- You will be more caring for others.

As I conclude this chapter, I hope it has been obvious that I made no attempt to convert you to my Christian way of thinking. How you serve your God is your choice. The methods of your worship are completely up to you. I do, however, hope that I have shown you the value of worship and the positive ways it can enhance your life in quality of experience and quantity of years.

Before moving onto the next chapter, take a few minutes to contemplate the state of your own spiritual wellness and to consider what you would be willing to do to make improvements in it. The following table contains a list of tactics effective in improving spiritual wellness. Consider the list carefully and in the space to the left of each tactic, write in a target date by which you plan to start using that tactic in your own life. As in most things in life, the choice is yours.

MY SPIRITUAL WELLNESS IMPROVEMENT PLAN	
DATE	SPIRITUAL WELLNESS IMPROVEMENT TACTICS
	Put your faith in a higher power, often thought of as God, outside of yourself.
	Set aside time, every day for worship, praise and expressions of thanksgiving.
	Find common ground with fellow believers by joining the church, synagogue, mosque, temple or any spiritual organization that meets your unique needs.
	Pray and or meditate each day being sure to fous not only on your needs but those things for which you are thankful.
	Read spiritually oriented material.
	Seek to understand and determine to respect religious differences.
	Discuss your faith with others who are interested and willing.
	Commit to memory spiritually uplifting material.

CHAPTER 8:
INTELLECTUAL WELLNESS:
EXPAND YOUR BRAINPOWER THROUGH LIFELONG LEARNING

> **Expand your intellect:**
>
> 1. *To become or make something become larger in size, scope, or extent, or greater in number or amount*
>
> 2. *To increase or cause something to increase in size or volume*
>
> 3. *Intelligence and knowledge: having a highly developed ability to think, reason, and understand, especially in combination with wide knowledge*

Several years ago, a TV commercial promoting college scholarship funding conveyed a timeless and important message: a mind is a terrible thing to waste. One of the saddest and most unnecessary consequences of the aging process is that minds, honed to razor sharpness through years of productive and often cutting edge labor, are allowed to go to sleep, beginning with an event called retirement. Those minds too, are a terrible thing to waste.

If you park a perfectly good car in your driveway and let it sit for years, doing nothing with or to it, it will rust, its tires will flatten, and ultimately it will battle your attempts to start it. Just as an unused car deteriorates, an unused mind fed only with the pabulum of Sunday football and afternoon soap operas rusts and fades too.

EMPOWERED POSSIBILITIES

Retired or not, never stop using your mind. Whether you are actively employed or happily retired, feed your mind something new every day. Never stop learning, experimenting, and trying new things until the day you die. A mind truly is a terrible thing to waste; especially if the mind being wasted is yours.

For most people, and soon I'll share with you a statistic to illustrate what I mean, loss of thinking and reasoning capacity does not have to accompany advanced age. That it often does is much more likely the result of mental inactivity than it is unavoidable age generated deterioration. Your mind and your muscles are two elements of your body that must be used in challenging ways in order to stay strong, resilient, and sharp.

While it is true that as many as ten thousand neurons die in the brain every day that represents no problem. Few if any of us use our brains efficiently anyway, so we can lose all those neurons and still function. There is further good news. Just as exercising the body will build new muscles, recent research shows that exercising the brain will build new neurons.

If forgetfulness is a sign of encroaching senility, then I'm in deep, deep trouble and have been for most of my life. Let me share with you a mental lapse experienced about seven years ago when, still in my fifties, I was young. Had I been ten years older when it happened, I've no doubt my friends and family would have been concerned about my approaching senility.

Occasionally, my longtime friend Gary Skilton and I enjoy meeting at First Watch, a favorite breakfast Mecca near his office. After one such pleasant and rewarding interaction with my favorite omelet and friend Gary of course, I paid the bill and headed to my car. In the act of inserting my key in the lock, I noticed my reflection in the

> **Intellectual Wellness:** To be wholly well involves expanding and preserving mental acuity.

EMPOWERED POSSIBILITIES

window. I was not wearing my glasses. I'm in the habit of taking them off while eating, and leaving them at the table wasn't a new experience for me. Many are the waiter who earns an extra tip for chasing me down in the parking lot, waving my glasses at me as he runs. This time, however, there was no jogging waiter coming to my rescue. Chuckling to myself, I headed back inside.

As I approached what had been our table, I caught the eye of the host. Even as I let him know I'd forgotten my glasses, I couldn't help noticing a strange look furl his brow. The glasses were not on the table.

I approached the host, re-explained my need, and asked him if he would be so kind as to check with the kitchen in the event that my glasses came in with the dirty dishes. Again, a strange look crossed his face, but he quickly, willingly, and silently entered the kitchen in search of my glasses. As I waited, I noticed a slight and bothersome obstruction to my peripheral vision, something not unlike a stray hair. Reaching to swipe it away, I discovered that I was wearing my glasses. This time laughing out loud at myself, I hurried from the restaurant without giving the host another chance to wonder about my sanity.

My friend Gary, by the way, who was already well on his way to work, is a recognized genius in the financial world. In the mundane world of everyday living however, he is helpless without his wife and assistant. Yet nobody, well hardly anybody who knows him, accuses him of being senile. It's possible that our mutual friend Gary Schultz does. But that's a serious case of "look who's talking."

For me, those brief memory hiccups aren't as rare in my life as I might wish. In the matter of the glasses, I've concluded that I carried them from the restaurant to my car during my first attempted exit. They weren't on when I saw my reflection in the window; really they weren't. But like so many things in my life, and not just in my life but in the lives of nearly everyone who wears them, putting my glasses on and taking them off are mostly unconscious and reflexive acts. I must've put them on as I walked back into the restaurant. I'm grateful that the parents of my young host raised him to be respectful to his elders even when they don't seem to deserve it.

> **Wisdom seldom comes without age but age often comes alone.**

Even as I chuckle at the memory, I'm reminded of my high school English teacher, Edna Lodge. She was a very good English teacher even though most of us didn't think so at the time. Thanks to her, I know something about poetry and can actually recite all or parts of several classic poems including that timeless epic Gray's "Elegy Written in a Country Churchyard." Also, thanks to her, I discovered the ability to write poetry. But with her being at about the age then that I am now, although blessed with the capacity to be an excellent English teacher and a credible librarian, Mrs. Lodge could be forgetful.

Not known for her patience, one day in English class, her frustration reached critical mass with our barely stifled laughter as she searched for her glasses. So angry was she that she stormed out of the classroom accusing us of hiding her glasses from her. She returned in less than two minutes, subdued but not apologetic. In her brief absence from the classroom, she discovered what we all knew. Her glasses, attached to her person with a decorative cord, had been propped up on her head slightly out of her line of sight. Just as my incident with lost glasses cannot be interpreted as an example of approaching senility, neither could hers. I must confess, however, that had we all known, as sixteen-year-olds, or even understood the concept of senility in the innocent days of 1964, it's what we would've called her—and we would've been wrong.

EMPOWERED POSSIBILITIES

I have believed, and probably you have too, that as I age, I must of necessity expect some decline in my mental acuity. Within the last two years, fortunately, I've discovered that's not necessarily true. The fact is, and I think you'll see it for yourself by the time you reach the end of this chapter, that most loss of mental acuity in older people is more the result of lack of mental stimulation than it is any inherent and unavoidable decline as part of the aging process.

At a conference on aging in Washington, DC, in the spring of 2009, I learned some interesting, exciting, and challenging facts. I've spent all but six years of my post-college career serving the aging population. Currently I am the Chief Executive Officer of a company called Waterman Communities, Inc. The average age of the population we serve is eighty-five. I learned that day in 2009 that according to research, 50 percent of people aged eighty-five and older (that's 50 percent of the people I serve) will experience some form of mental deterioration, including Alzheimer's disease and other forms of dementia. The good news is, most don't have to.

Considering the size of the baby boomer population, the potential Alzheimer's population carries tremendous opportunity for developing business models centered on serving people with memory loss. Serving the Alzheimer's population is exciting in the creativity it affords. But if there is a way to postpone, mitigate, or even prevent mental deterioration, I'm on board. Hidden in the rest of the statistical report lies a vast opportunity that really gets me excited.

Of those 50 percent who are susceptible to loss of mental acuity, only 37 percent exhibit organic causes. That means that there is a strong probability that nearly two-thirds of the older people you know who seem to be losing it mentally, may not have to. If there is no organic cause, no disease, no chemical deterioration in the brain causing this loss of mental acuity, then it stands to reason

EMPOWERED POSSIBILITIES

that not only can memory in the aged be improved, but the symptoms of dementia, including those that look like Alzheimer's, might just be preventable. If not preventable, then they are certainly reducible. While it is true that the aging brain shrinks in size, so vast is its potential and so slight is its utilization even at peak productivity that this loss in size does not have to translate into loss of reasoning capacity.

> **The Myth:** *The older you get, the more forgetful you become, and there isn't much you can do about it.* **The Facts:** *A regular program of physical fitness combined with constant exploration and learning can, for most of us, keep our minds as sharp as ever they were.*

As a senior service professional, I have been, and remain, staunchly committed to providing memory care services. Since that early spring day in Washington, DC, however, my concept of what those services should be has expanded into the realms of mitigation and prevention.

Very simply, the majority of older people who suffer from loss of mental acuity don't have to, and the antidote is continued learning, exploring, experimenting, and trying new things combined with physical exercise. Yes, couch potatoes, physical exercise will increase and protect your capacity to enjoy those soap operas and sporting events you so thrive on.

> *Everyone has a risk muscle. You keep it in shape by trying new things. If you don't, it atrophies. Make a point of using it at least once a day.*
>
> **Roger Von Oeck**

In fact, it just may be that our children are on to something good with their videogame obsession. As it turns out, challenging games such as crossword puzzles, Sudoku, Trivial Pursuit, Jeopardy, Wheel of Fortune, and various forms of word puzzles can serve to keep us sharp mentally. The element our children so often overlook, however, is the need for balance. Once again it must be said, successful living at any age requires a proper mix of physical and mental exercise. While texting will build strong thumbs and video games, sharp vision, the human mind and body have so much more to offer. Much better than video and other mind challenging games however, are learning new languages and new skills, and taking college-level courses in subjects that are new and interesting to develop skills that can be used beyond the video screen.

As previously stated, for a full definition of good health, both the mind and the body must be in peak working condition. Recent research clearly establishes the link between physical fitness and brain function. The reason is simple and actually quite obvious. Physical activity improves blood flow to the brain. Increased blood flow sharpens mental acuity. The good news for all of you couch potatoes is that you don't have to become an extreme athlete to enjoy the benefits of exercise-driven, improved brain function. A daily walk, as described in an earlier chapter, will do quite nicely.

It should be comforting, at this point, to realize that just as lack of exercise will cause your body to go soft, so too will the lack of intellectual exercise cause your brain and thinking capacity to go soft. The comfort of course, lies in the fact that not only can you exercise your body; you can also exercise your brain.

While physical exercise is critical to your ability to stay mentally sharp, specific exercises for the brain are also necessary. Perhaps you will find the following three types of brain exercises to be helpful.

The one thing that even the most scientifically illiterate human being knows about the brain is that it's divided into two halves, referred to as the right brain and the left brain. Much of our personality is determined by which half of the brain we use the most.

EMPOWERED POSSIBILITIES

The left brain is the source of factual reasoning, and language and math skills. People with a left-brain label tend to be objective in their reasoning. Science and math come easily for them. Decisions are fact-based, with little thought given to feelings and emotions.

> Don't fear failure so much that you refuse to try new things. The saddest summary of a life contains three descriptions: could have, might have, and should have.

Effective left-brain workouts include learning a new language, acquiring a new set of technical skills, and/or simply playing such mentally challenging games as Sudoku and crossword puzzles.

The right side of your brain is the source of creativity and emotion-based reasoning. Right-brained individuals are known for their ability to think outside of the box. In fact, a strongly right-brained individual may never even have noticed that there is a box.

To stimulate the right side of your brain—and you should do this if your usual strengths are left-brain oriented—try something creative, such as learning a musical instrument you've never played before, getting better at an instrument you have played before, taking up a new craft or hobby, or simply joining a choir. In fact, at this very moment, I find myself turning to look at my seldom-used karaoke machine. Maybe I, at the age of sixty-three, should go after that rock star career after all.

> Physical exercise is good for you, and so is mental exercise. The brain is remarkably "plastic" even into old age. This means that new connections can be formed between brain cells at any age. You can stimulate this type of growth by doing new things.

For a general, overall brain workout, try meditation. In the chapter on worship we considered the benefits of meditation in its ability to reduce stress and anxiety. As stress and anxiety decline, the brain is left free to focus on happiness and contentment. That simply has to be good for the brain.

Consider reading. Reading is much more than a source of information or a pastime. Reading is one of the most effective ways to stimulate your brain. That's because the act of reading causes your brain to formulate mental pictures of the subject matter, thus increasing the flow of your creative juices.

In this high-tech world, the written, hardcover book and actual "hold and fold in your hands" newspaper are at high risk of going the way of the dinosaur. Just this past week my cousin Willis, a teacher, sent around a cartoon clearly depicting the danger that traditional forms of reading might become a lost art. It pictured a man sitting forward in his chair holding a book, engaged in earnest conversation with a little girl who had just asked him what he was doing.

"It's called reading," he replied. "It's how we update the software in our brain."

Watching television is an activity that most people do but hardly anyone wants to admit to. Turn television into a mental exercise by playing along with trivia and other game shows. Educational programming is particularly good for brain stimulation.

Even your favorite drama can be a stimulating activity if you work along with the hero detective, trying to follow the clues and solve the crime. Now that I think about it, my wife and I have developed watching television as mental stimulation to an art form. She likes to multitask. Consequently, with her favorite programs running on the big screen, she is simultaneously on her laptop computer, surfing Facebook, e-mail, and the web with special emphasis on favorite shopping sites.

EMPOWERED POSSIBILITIES

Since I'm not an effective multi-tasker (*even now a certain much loved, favorite cooking pot sits soaking in the sink in an effort to overcome the negative effects of forgotten soup combined with stovetop heat while I tried to do other things*), my job is to pay close attention to the storyline so that I can explain the action to her when she asks for it. Maybe you and your spouse or significant other are practiced at this form of mental stimulation too. If so, and you are the one designated to follow the storyline, redirect that frustration you're tempted to feel when the multi-tasker checks in for an update at the most exciting spot in the story, into a sense of appreciation for the exercise your brain is getting.

Do you remember those school days when teachers liked to give us what sometimes seemed like entire books to memorize? It turns out that memorization is also good for total brain health. I have often thought about but never actually memorized President Lincoln's Gettysburg Address. Maybe now is the time.

One of the most pleasant forms of brain exercise is social activity. There is a clearly defined connection between an active social calendar and a productively busy, enduringly healthy brain.

Change some routines. About five years ago, it occurred to me that I'd been driving to work by the same route, almost without exception, for nearly ten years. I wish I could say that it was a desire to be more creative that motivated me to start exploring new routes, but I can't. The Orange County, Florida, school district built a brand new school and recreation complex right in the middle of one of the most beautiful tree-lined hillsides I had been driving by and enjoying for those ten years. It's a great school—my granddaughter Riley goes there, and the recreational complex is as well designed as any I've ever seen. Working together, the two did not destroy my scenic vistas, but merely changed them. What motivated me to seek other routes was the new and much lower speed limit that came with the school.

EMPOWERED POSSIBILITIES

As a result, I now know at least six different ways to drive to work and can proudly report my ability to completely avoid major highways. Further, no route takes more than five minutes longer than the traffic light laden, although most common, route that follows the always busy, four-lane Highway 441. In the process, I discovered yet another tip for strengthening total brain capacity: shake up your routine! Explore new routes as I did. Try out that new restaurant you've been hearing about. Pursue positive change. It's good for the brain.

In a previous chapter we discussed the physical health benefits of exercise. We clearly established that an individual is virtually never too old to increase muscle mass and therefore strength. Now we can see that not only will exercise increase physical capacity, it also strengthens your brain. Just as an exercise as simple as a daily walk greatly increases your energy and physical capacity, that same simple walk is also sharpening your brain's ability to think. That's just about the best two-for-one offer you can find. Take a walk and in the process, strengthen both your body and your brain. How can you beat a deal like that? Get stronger and smarter at the same time.

Possibly the thing you will struggle with most as you seek to maximize your mental health is just how to reduce the stress in your life. Stress not only strains your heart but makes your brain go fuzzy too.

Growing up, I, as I'm sure you did to, often heard the expression "you are what you eat." We believe it even if we don't practice it. Even that individual with the most overpowering urge for junk food knows that a plate of vegetables would be far better for him or her than that tantalizing bag of chips currently gripped in his/her sweaty fingers. But even in the knowing there is denial. The chips will be eaten and the guilt, over time, minimized.

EMPOWERED POSSIBILITIES

Recent research complicates the matter even further. We now are learning that not only will the proper food strengthen our bodies, but eating right can also strengthen our minds.

While over the next few paragraphs I will report the connection between what you eat and how well you think, I must add a strong disclaimer. I personally have discovered none of the facts I'm about to share. I'm not a scientist. In high school I only took two science classes. The first was biology and I scored a solid C. The second was chemistry and I barely made a C and even then only because of the generous spirit of my lab partner. In college, my only science course was nutrition. I loved food even then. I still love food today, and that includes all manner of chips, nearly every form of pie, a passion for Tollhouse chocolate chip cookies—as an aside, I do like walnuts in them and walnuts are very good for your brain, and a none too secret love affair with moist chocolate cake. Yet I am taking the information I'm about to share very seriously, and I hope you will too. After all, I got all this information from my good friend Google, and Google wouldn't lie.

> *No diet will remove all the fat from your body because the brain is entirely fat. Without a brain you might look good, but all you could do is run for public office.*
>
> **George Bernard Shaw**

First, let me give you the simplest possible guideline. Build your diet around a wide variety of fruits and vegetables. Fresh is the best and raw can't be beat. Having said that, most of the fruit I eat is frozen and I really like cooked, well-seasoned vegetables. I do eat the fresh and raw stuff too though, and I doubt that the frozen fruit and cooked vegetables are hurting me in any substantial way.

Now for some more detail. The best place to start is a short discussion on fats. Not all fat is bad for you. In fact, some fats are

EMPOWERED POSSIBILITIES

absolutely essential for good health. The group of fats most often recommended is known as Omega three fatty acids. These can be found in fish, most notably salmon. If you don't like to eat fish, however, your local health food store can supply you with omega-3 fatty acid supplements served up in capsule or pill form, even flavored if you need them to be.

You're used to hearing that saturated fats are bad for your heart. You know that olive oil is much better for you than lard. The good news for those of you who don't want to learn any more than you absolutely have to, is that the same fats that are bad for your heart are also bad for your brain. Therefore, if you cook with monounsaturated fats like olive oil you will improve the health of your heart, your body, and your brain. You will then, in fact, be well on your way to eating the much vaunted Mediterranean diet so frequently linked to better heart health.

Nuts provide excellent sources of not only energy enhancing protein but also mentally stimulating fatty acids. The walnut particularly has been linked to improved brain health. In fact, and I didn't learn this from Google, eating seven to eight walnut halves per day satisfies your body's need for omega-3 fats. That is the only reason, I can assure you, why I like walnuts in my Tollhouse chocolate chip cookies. Did I mention that walnut laden chocolate chip cookies are especially good for you when taken with milk? Ideally that milk would be fat free, but I can't drink that. It looks like the water in the cleaning bucket after your teacher made you wash the erasers. If you like it, however, go for it.

This next diet tip might not only surprise you but discourage you a little bit as well. Curry may very well reduce the risk of dementia. In a study administered by the national University of Singapore, it was shown that people who regularly ate curry had a much lower rate of dementia. While curry can take many different forms, those that contain turmeric, a proven anti-inflammatory factor, seem to be the best. The reason is that turmeric contains high

EMPOWERED POSSIBILITIES

levels of curcumin, a substance of which I have never heard but am now glad to know about. Other spices in curries that also prove helpful include ginger, cinnamon, and garlic. I for one will be eating more Indian food. I even have a $50 gift certificate for my favorite Indian restaurant. Will you give it a try?

Blueberries, the dominant ingredient in my second most favorite pie (cherry is number one), contain some of the highest levels of antioxidants to be found in any fruit. What I know about antioxidants, minimal as it is, I've already shared. The knowledge that it's beneficial, that it can be found in walnuts and that walnuts occasionally make their way into my chocolate chip cookies and smoothies, and that it keeps your brain from rusting, is more than enough information for me. If you want to know more, you'll have to look it up yourself. Anyway, looking the information up will be a helpful and mentally stimulating activity for you.

Animal studies have shown that adding blueberries to the diet improves learning ability and memory retention. Now I understand why my dog, Sable, gets so excited when I add the blueberries to my smoothie mix. For a long time I've avoided giving her blueberries because even frozen, they are a very messy fruit. Since learning of their benefits however, I occasionally add dried blueberries to her dog food. She seems to like them and though it could be my imagination, I do notice an extra spring in her step and sharpness in her eye.

A Japanese study found that people who drank two cups of green tea per day had a much lower risk for dementia then did people who drank less than three cups a week. The bad news for you coffee and English tea drinkers is that coffee and black tea didn't produce the same results.

It's only common sense, and in fact I've already made it clear, that your diet should be your main source of nutrients. However, some people just don't like vegetables and either can't or won't

EMPOWERED POSSIBILITIES

learn how. Others might be looking for a little extra boost. In either case, you might consider some or all of the following supplements.

1. The benefits of fish oil have already been covered.

2. Ginkgo Biloba is often trumpeted as a memory aid. It may, in fact, have moderate effectiveness, thanks to its apparent ability to improve blood flow. At the very least, it has never been shown to harm anyone.

3. Curcumin, that magical, memory-enhancing element found in some curries, is available in supplement form for those who just can't get into curry.

4. Three other supplements with hard to pronounce names are alpha lipoic acid, acetyl carnitine and phosphatidylserine; even spell check was stumped on that last one. The first two taken together seem to protect the brain from age-related damage. The third one, whose name is so hard I won't even try to spell it again, increases acetylcholine levels in the brain (also hard to spell and pronounce). This little powerhouse has been shown to be effective in both animal and human studies, though in what ways I'm not exactly sure.

By now, you know I'm not a big fan of supplements. It has always seemed to me that supplements can get out of control and you end up spending half your morning just swallowing pills. So my personal main thrust in using diet to improve my mental capacity focuses on olive oil, Indian food, salmon, blueberries, and green tea. But if you like swallowing pills, then dietary supplements can work for you. And remember, almost everything you do to increase your physical strength will, at the same time, improve your mental capacity and vice versa.

EMPOWERED POSSIBILITIES

Before you move on to the next chapter, take a few moments to consider the actions that you are willing to take to improve your mental acuity. In the table below, you will find a list of the various mind-improving tactics I've shared with you in this chapter. Please review the list and in the space to the left of each tactic, enter the date on which you propose to implement that tactic in your pursuit of better, stronger, and longer lasting mental acuity.

MY MENTAL ACUITY IMPROVEMENT PLAN	
DATE	MENTAL ACUITY IMPROVEMENT TACTIC
	Start a regular exercise program that I can manage, enjoy and stick to
	Learn a new language
	Play challenging games such as crosswords, jigsaw puzzles and Sudoku
	Learn new skills
	Take up art or music lessons
	Develop a new hobby
	Read
	Memorize favorite poems, Bible texts and/or speeches
	Avoid saturated fats
	Start eating brain and body health food
	Take supplements

CHAPTER 9: SOCIAL WELLNESS:
BUILD AND MAINTAIN POSITIVE RELATIONSHIPS

> **Positive Relationships:**
>
> **Relating to other people in positive, productive, and energizing ways for the purpose of:**
> 1. **Connection**
> 2. **Affiliation**
> 3. **Rapport**
> 4. **Bonding**
> 5. **Linking and**
> 6. **Associating**

The final letter in our EMPOWER acronym is the letter R, representing relationships. Regardless of whether you believe in Creation, the Big Bang theory, or some other form of evolution, it's quite clear that human beings are meant to be social. In fact, most humans crave and even need social interaction. The few who don't can be very scary individuals and therefore the subject of another book that I shall probably never write.

The quality of our relationships determines the value and effectiveness of our social and business networks. Without strong, connecting relationships, little progress toward any goal, large or small, personal or business, would be possible.

EMPOWERED POSSIBILITIES

Relationships are the foundation on which we erect our awareness and understanding of community, family, and home. Few relationships of any depth or value fail to lead to friendship, with its focus on responsiveness and caring. In using the word friendship here, I'm suggesting that there needs to be positive friendship, even and probably especially, among family members.

It's difficult for me, a social individual to my core, to imagine a life without relationships. I don't have a long list of friends, but each name on my friendship list is special, loved, and valued by me. In fact, the older I get, the more I find I want to physically be with the individuals I most care about, as often as I can. Many of them live hundreds even thousands of miles away. More and more I find myself on airplanes and behind the wheel of my car traveling to see them. In fact, if any of you reading this book identify yourself as one of my current or long-lost friends, expect a visit from me in the not-too-distant future. While I'd love for you to visit me in Florida where my thoroughly empty nested house offers three guest bedrooms and two guest bathrooms, I value our relationship so much that I really don't mind coming to you. Just let me know where you are and I'll put you on my travel schedule.

At the office, I much prefer to leave the comfort of my executive chair and walk to the offices of the colleagues whose input I might want at a particular point in time. I prefer face-to-face contact, and besides, the walk is aerobic.

I've been receiving and benefiting from chiropractic treatment for four years now. In the process, in ways that are mysterious to me as well as to her, I've become one of several father figures in Dr. Ramah's life. Along with her own father, we each perform a slightly different fatherly function for her. We're part of what she calls her brain trust. I've even been known, on occasion, to make a chiropractic appointment, not so much because I felt my body needed adjustment, but because I find that her hectic lifestyle

EMPOWERED POSSIBILITIES

and machine gun intellect energize, entertain, and amuse me at a value well beyond the cost of the office visit.

Also, sometimes I go because I suspect she needs to talk to me, and I'm usually right. Shouldn't friends do that for one another? I leave her office feeling better physically, and I'd like to believe that most of the time I've helped her think through a current challenge. We have, I believe, helped each other a lot over the past four years. Ramah is well worth the cost of her services. Consequently, even after the most mutually beneficial of visits, money always and without exception leaves my pocket and goes straight to hers.

Well, there was that one time when the money flowed my way. We made a bet that she couldn't go two weeks without taking work home. My side of the bet involved avoiding desserts for the same length of time. I succeeded. She didn't. She lost and paid up without argument, and I happily took her money.

Over the long haul however, what I've spent has been well worth it, and I think the benefits to each of us are substantial, though weighted far more heavily on my side. In fact, the motivation to write this book comes in no small part from some clarification sessions she conducted with me. Thanks to Ramah's work, the scientific basis of which I can't begin to understand, I finish far more started projects than ever before in my life. It's important to let your friends know you appreciate them, so thank you Ramah. I appreciate you for your professional competence, contagious enthusiasm, and insatiable thirst for knowledge and self-improvement, but most of all for granting me the honor of being your friend as well as your patient.

I have a desk lamp poised just above my computer screen; nothing unusual about that except that each time I turn it on, I think of Ramah. I'm not sure when it began or why, except that her work with me has turned on a few lights in my life such as the strength and focus to finish this book. By the way Ramah, you have a new light in your own life, and I wish you and Fabian many years of happiness and success together. You both, in my opinion, have chosen wisely.

The best relationships are mutually beneficial. A one-sided relationship with one party doing all of the giving and the other party doing all the receiving may be necessary for a time. Perhaps one party to the relationship is in a particularly bad situation and in need of a high-level of support. It is not, however, a good relationship if it stays that way forever. Relationships, in order to survive, grow, and stand the test of time, must be two-way streets.

Aside from social support, there are some solid business reasons for developing relationships. It's called networking, and the need for it never goes away. It's difficult to succeed in life, much less business, without a network of contacts to which you can go when you need direction and/or information.

Interestingly enough, I recently learned that the variety and diversity of your social connections is of more importance and value than the aggregate number. In other words,

> *Social Wellness: Relationships and a broad range of networks are essential to life success and whole-person wellness*

it's great to have one hundred friends but those friends are of more value to you if they are spread out among several different groups. If your church is large enough, you might be able to call one hundred of your fellow members friends. That is a good thing. But an even better thing is to have one hundred good friends spread out among your church, your Rotary club, your professional association, your fitness center, and your golfing club.

Did I actually include your golfing club on my list? For me, golf is just another four letter word better left unspoken in genteel company, but some of you haven't grown beyond its addictive

EMPOWERED POSSIBILITIES

clutches so we'll leave it on the list. Keep this in mind however: when looking for advice, you need the truth, and the risk attached to seeking advice from your fellow golfers is that you are too used to lying to each other. Mulligans, helpful in computing golfing scores, don't always work well in real life.

The problem with limiting your social connections to one group is that you all know the same people with access to the same answers. By having contacts and connections through a variety of organizations you open up a virtually endless supply of sources when you need advice, resources, and/or answers.

While marriage can and frequently does test the limits of human patience and endurance, research shows that married people and/or people with a live-in companion are happier and healthier than are those who live alone.

As we've already said, death is part of the aging process. The choice is not whether you will die but to a large extent, when and how. Death almost always has a serious, negative impact on relationships. Is there no end to my gift for profound statements? Death robs us, often at the worst possible times, of our most valued connections, and the death of a spouse carries the most serious negative consequences of all.

More than a dozen years ago a long married couple (part of an endless line of long married couples), moved into the senior living facility where I am currently the Chief Executive Officer. Though they'd been married for well over fifty years, they opted for a life without children. College professors by profession and intellectuals by nature, they satisfied their social needs with their own companionship and that of a limited number of friends who shared their common and sometimes unusual interests.

One of their first quests shortly after moving in was a search for another couple to play Scrabble, in French. Neither one of them

EMPOWERED POSSIBILITIES

had brothers or sisters, so there were no caring and interested nieces and nephews.

Sadly, the Mrs., who clearly captained their marital ship, passed away, leaving the husband to fend for himself, something he was completely unused to doing.

About four months after the death of his wife, the husband informed me that he would soon remarry. He went on to relate that several of his friends felt he hadn't allowed enough time to pass after the death of his wife. His response to these friends is worth sharing. His exact words were, "I feel that at my age, if you don't have to live alone, why should you?"

Nearly ten years have passed since he shared that bit of wisdom with me, and both he and his new wife are gone. His legacy, however, valuable to me and I hope that since I'm sharing it with you, valuable to you as well, lies in that thought. Why should you be alone, if you don't have to be?

As a further point of interest, even though it was only the second marriage for him, it was at least the third if not the fourth for his second wife. Apparently she, too, believed that if you didn't have to be alone, you shouldn't be.

This couple, I find, are by no means unique in the aging population. I know one lusty lady in her nineties, currently married to her fifth husband, who has made it clear that should anything happen to him there will be a number six. She, by the way, is only number two for her number five. Did you follow those numbers?

> **The Myth:** *The older you get, the more likely it will be that you will have increasingly fewer good relationships.* **The Facts:** *Relationships do change with age. Old friends die. People who age successfully simply make new friends.*

EMPOWERED POSSIBILITIES

A courtly gentleman nonagenarian of my acquaintance is energetically embarked on his third marriage. He is husband number four for her. I don't think I've ever seen a happier, more romantically loving couple than those two. Furthermore, their children, spawned with preceding spouses, are also quite happy with their new stepparents. In fact, the gentleman tells me with a distinct chuckle in his voice, that even though the two of them have no children together, they keep trying. I'll leave you, the reader, to put your own spin on that.

While family dynamics have been studied for decades, research into the health impact of friendship and social networking is a fairly recent interest. Often, the results are so striking that one researcher confidently claimed that friendships have a more positive impact on psychological health (*and therefore, I think, physical health*) than family relationships.

This insight is particularly of interest to me, and if you'll permit me, I'd like to address issues of specific interest to senior citizens, before discussing general relationship principles. I've long believed that it is far better for older people to remain in the community they are used to living in, connected with, and like, surrounded by good friends, than to uproot them to live near their families. In my experience, friends, particularly friends of a similar age, tend to have more time for you and more interests in common with you than do most relatives.

It isn't that friends love you more than relatives do; it's just that friends tend to be less judgmental, far more tolerant, and therefore more supportive than family members. Also, if you are old and retired, and have built a life filled with friends who are also older and retired, they have more time for you than do your busy and involved children. Your children love you, but they will grossly underestimate the amount of time and attention you're used to and need.

EMPOWERED POSSIBILITIES

I personally and sadly experienced this truth with my own mother. In the year 1999 she told me of her plans to move from Nebraska back to Illinois to be near her daughter, my sister. Nebraska had been her home for over twenty years, because it was my father's native state. His friends became hers. His family firmly embraced her, according her undisputed, favorite aunt status. Central Nebraska, specifically the town of Gothenburg where she lived, was filled with nieces and nephews, brothers and sisters from my father's side who had long considered her a member of the family. Always one to make friends easily, my mother knew everyone in her close-knit senior community.

But she wanted to reconnect with her daughter, and my sister shared her dreams. Both envisioned shopping trips and nostalgic rides filled with old memories, to favorite haunts revisited together as they rebuilt their mother/daughter bonds. What both failed to appreciate, and sadly I did to, was that the robust, active, and still employed mother who loved playing softball with her grandchildren, and who moved to Nebraska twenty years earlier, was at best a dim shadow barely recognizable in the old, overweight, diabetic, often crotchety and too long sedentary senior who took her place.

My mother missed Gothenburg, Nebraska, and the many family and friends who loved her. That my sister loved her to too is not in dispute. But my sister was one person with a husband, children, pets, a mother-in-law, and a house to look after. In Nebraska, there were at least ten nieces and nephews, a half a dozen grand nieces and nephews, a brother-in-law, three sisters-in-law, and the administration and entire population of her retirement community in her support system.

The downtown merchants all knew her by name. Her favorite restaurants were just a few blocks away and there was always an available niece or nephew to take her out when she wanted to go. Her car, though she seldom chose to drive it, sat just outside her door a tangible symbol of independence and an available mode of transportation should her niece or nephew of choice not have one of his or her own.

I wish, when she asked, that I would've agreed to move her back to Nebraska. I found out, just this past summer, that she called one of my cousins and asked if she could live with him. I refused to move her for what I thought were good reasons. In Illinois, the state provided her with a prescription drug plan at very little cost. In Nebraska, I was her drug plan. For me at the time, it was a purely financial decision. My son was, after all, early in his educational trek through a variety of colleges, most of them expensive, and my wife and I were the sources of his full scholarship.

I suspect, and though my sister and I both blame ourselves to some extent, that her decision to leave her large support system to be near her daughter was a downsizing decision she shouldn't have made. She loved my sister and my sister loved her, but in the end, exchanging a support system of nearly thirty in number who did not share her blood, to be near my sister who did, was not enough.

In the early morning hours of Saturday, May 18, 2001, surrounded by neighbors she barely knew with my sister only five miles away, my mother had the heart attack from which she couldn't recover. As far as we can tell, her last conscious act was the activation of her lifeline button in an effort to summon help, help that didn't arrive in time.

I can only estimate, based on my experience, that had mom stayed in her familiar community supported by her many friends and adopted family, she would've enjoyed a longer life. True, there may not have been any blood ties, but the love ties that did exist were strong indeed. That she didn't stay was no one's fault—not hers, not my sister's, and not mine. At the time of her decision, we all hoped and felt that it was right and good, but

EMPOWERED POSSIBILITIES

it wasn't. It was made in love and for the right reasons, but as a decision, it was wrong.

The simple fact is this. As you age and your needs increase, you may truly want to be near your family and they may sincerely want you with them too. I must admit, it often works out. But more often, it doesn't. When your roots are deep in a comfortable and nurturing community and your friendships are true and mutual, difficult as it may be to accept, most are better off living near their friends and enjoying visits from their children.

If you are living in a senior community, as was my mother, the community support systems are designed specifically to meet your needs. The same applies if you are a caring child concerned about an aging parent. Filling needs that can be difficult for time strapped children is the very heart and soul of business for a senior community. They are designed to do it, equipped to do it, and staffed to do it, and most do it very, very well.

Many realities in today's often-uncertain world, and its unpredictable economy, drive the recent increased tendency for children to move their parent, sometimes without offering them any choice, to be near them. The motivation is good and founded in love, but often misguided.

My sister and I learned the hard way that proximity to children was not as important as proximity to friends, nieces, nephews, brothers and sisters even if they had inherited her by marriage. When sick, who did she call? Not much to think about there—niece Peggy who lived only four blocks away, or niece Joyce, a nurse in the hospital next door.

> **Webster's 1828 definition of friendship is "one who has sufficient interest to serve another; genuine, pure, real, not counterfeit, adulterated or false. True friendship is a noble and virtuous attachment, springing from a pure source, a respect for worth or amiable qualities."**

EMPOWERED POSSIBILITIES

Who managed her finances for her? Her highly organized niece, Onna did. When she needed a ride, who stepped to the plate? Niece Nancy was always ready for a shopping excursion or an impromptu meal out. When she needed companionship for an evening of TV, her soft-spoken nephew Bob dropped by. When any special services were needed, she simply approached the administration in her senior living complex. Even the nuns from the small convent, friends from her days in Oconto, a small town about thirty miles from Gothenburg, stayed in touch. Neighbor children, who learned to bake cookies in her kitchen, called, wrote, and visited often.

Building friendships is a healing tool every bit as powerful as the best treatments modern medicine has to offer and the most potent drugs your doctor can prescribe. The research, to back up my statement, is broad-based and plentiful, and supports the following points about the health benefits of friendship.

During the ten-year course of one study, older people with a large circle of friends died at a much lower rate than did those participating in the study who had few friends.

You're going to love this one. I have long believed that the type of people we associate with has a great impact on the kind of people we become ourselves. After all, how different can a person be from their friends? A large study conducted in 2007 suggests that people whose close friends gain weight are at much greater risk of gaining weight themselves. I guess the point is this. If you want to lose weight, make sure there are at least a few thin people in your circle of friends for you to look to as role models.

Another recently conducted study illustrates that strong social ties promote brain health as we age. While at first possibly surprising, upon further reflection this point is really quite obvious. Contact with friends leads to conversations and other shared activities, all of which tend to be mentally stimulating. As mentally stimulating as challenging games like crossword puzzles and Sudoku can be, regular, social interaction is superior. Even better, combine the two: play challenging games with your friends.

Reaching out to friends is often more beneficial in the healing process than reaching out to family. Friends, it seems, are less judgmental and therefore a greater source of support and encouragement.

The Gallup organization quite possibly knows more about how to create an effective teamwork environment than anyone else. They've identified friendship as one of the key elements for an effective and satisfying workplace. I believe friendship is just as necessary to an effective and satisfying lifestyle beyond the workplace. I wonder if this is what the wise King Solomon had in mind when he wrote the following in Proverbs 18:24: *A man that hath friends must shew himself friendly: and there is a friend that sticketh closer than a brother.* KJV

A study involving nurses with breast cancer made this startling discovery: women with ten or more close friends were four times less likely to die from their cancer than women with few or no friends. An interesting side note to this study is the fact that the key to healing was the simple fact of having friends. The amount of contact didn't seem to matter. Furthermore, and I'm not quite sure what to make of this, having a spouse didn't seem to have any impact on potential for survival at all. You can analyze this last fact further if you wish. As for me, it's a road I don't plan to travel anytime soon.

Lower stress levels in people with strong social networks may be, in part, the reason why socially connected people are less likely to suffer from colds. As I write this, I'm in what I hope are the final hours of a fifteen-day struggle with my first real cold in three years. I think I need to make more friends.

EMPOWERED POSSIBILITIES

Apparently facing challenge in the company of good friends can make you less fearful. In a seemingly simple study, small groups of students, equipped with weighted backpacks, were placed at the base of a hill and asked to estimate its steepness as a prelude to climbing it. It was found that students standing next to friends judged the hill to be less steep and therefore easier to climb than did the members of those small groups who were not friends. Also, the longer the duration of the friendship, the less challenging the hill seemed. Could it be that old friends are the truest and the best? Certainly, meeting life obstacles with the support and companionship of friends leads to much greater success.

We haven't yet figured out why or how, but strong friendships strengthen your immune system and reduce your stress levels. Having a friend along, if only for moral support, gives you hope and faith that things will turn out OK. The support of a good friend in the face of a challenge lowers your blood pressure and reduces your heart rate. Your friends can keep you motivated and energized even in the most difficult of circumstances.

One way you can enhance your friendships is to add laughter and humor to them.

Humor and playful communication strengthen our relationships by triggering positive feelings and fostering emotional connection. When we laugh together, a positive bond is created. This bond acts as a strong buffer against stress, disagreements, and disappointment. Laughing with others is more powerful than laughing alone.

Sharing laughter is one of the most effective tools for keeping relationships fresh and fun. All emotional sharing can build strong and lasting relationship bonds, but sharing laughter and/or humor play adds joy, vitality, and resilience. Humor is a powerful and effective way to heal resentments, disagreements, and hurts. Laughter unites people during tough times.

EMPOWERED POSSIBILITIES

Mutual laughter and play are an essential components of strong, healthy relationships. By making a conscious effort to incorporate more humor and play into your daily interactions, you can improve the quality of your love relationships as well as your connections with co-workers, family members, and friends.

A good friend of mine and longtime resident in Waterman Village recently moved to an out-of-state senior community to be near her daughter. In our last conversation before she left, she assured me that she and her daughter were good friends. In her new community with her daughter close by, she was miserable. That misery only abated as she made new friends. She can do that because she's outgoing by nature and was well used to navigating the relationship waters of a retirement community. She would still be miserable, I truly believe, had she moved in with her daughter without easy access to new friendships.

If I had to guess why friends have a greater positive impact on health than do family members, my guess would be this. Your family is chosen arbitrarily before birth. While a relative may verbally disown you, actual disowning is physically impossible to do. Friends, on the other hand, are mutually chosen. For some reason, these facts make human beings less prone to hiding things from their friends. Consequently, communication between friends is often more open and honest that it is between family members.

A careful analysis of the past few paragraphs suggests the following:

1. People with a strong circle of supporting friendships tend to live longer than do those with few or no friends.

2. If your close friends gain weight, it is very likely that you will too. I wonder, then, if the reverse is also true. Will I be able to lose weight if I can just talk my close friends into going on a diet with me? This could be the

EMPOWERED POSSIBILITIES

key reason why Weight Watchers is still around and so successful after all these years. It's built on a model of social support, leading me to wonder how ultimately successful its more recent venture into online dieting will be. By the way Weight Watchers, thanks for what you helped Jennifer Hudson do!!!

3. Strong social ties will promote better brain health.

4. The support of friends is often a better source of healing and good feeling than the similar support of family members, and that includes the spouse.

5. Individuals with a strong social support system involving at least ten good friends are significantly less likely to die of a serious disease, including cancer.

6. Strong ties of friendship are important factors in stress reduction.

7. Facing challenge in the company of friends seems to make us braver and potentially more effective in dealing with the challenge.

8. Good friendships boost your immune system and lead to a longer, healthier life.

9. Having friends makes your life more fun and easier to handle.

10. With good friends, you feel connected and therefore a more important part of the world around you.

11. Your friends often understand you better than your family does. Put simply, friends will usually put up with more of your nonsense than your family will.

12. You are more likely to get an honest opinion in the form of constructive criticism from a friend than from a family member.

13. Friends are good sources of motivation and energy.

Now that's an imposing list of benefits, and just think—they are all available to anyone with a strong social network of good, long-standing and supportive friends. How strong is your social network? An individual with friends enjoys the security of knowing there is always someone to turn to. Very simply, good friends make your life better. Whether you're dealing with stress, depression, loss, or recovering from a serious illness you will do it better and faster with friends. In fact, it has been suggested that not having friends is as damaging to your health as smoking and obesity.

Possibly by now you are thinking, as am I, that it would be nice to have more and better friends. But how do we go about doing that? The best way to make and keep friends is to be a good friend. Here are some tips for being a good friend that you just might find helpful.

1. **Spend time together.** In doing this, please note that the value comes from the quality of time more than quantity of time. While it's great to be able to spend long periods of time together basking in the benefits of your mutual friendship, it isn't always possible. Perhaps you're busy or your friend is busy. It may be that you're separated by distance. The good news is that even if regular personal contact is difficult, the telephone, e-mail, and even thoughtful cards sent the old-fashioned "snail mail" way are effective substitutes. You may not be able to visit often, but you can call and/or write often. With the benefits of Skype and other visual communication programs, access to a computer al-

lows you to cross the boundaries of the ether and visit face-to-face.

2. **Give your friends a high priority.** Sure it may be true that your house does need cleaning, your dog or cat may be a week or two beyond the need of a bath, and your pantry really is bare. There is always an errand to run or a chore to do, and there always will be. But thanks to life's many uncertainties, that friend you're thinking about right now might not always be there. I can't recall ever hearing anyone say, "I'm sorry I spent the day with my friend."

3. **Remember that a true friend is there in the good times and the bad.** Your presence at a funeral may be more important to your friend and their well-being than your presence at the wedding of their son or daughter. The opposite is also true. You should have no hesitation at all in calling on your true friends in your times of need. You are happy to have them at your son's wedding, but you need them and draw comfort from them at your spouse's funeral.

4. **Don't keep score.** Who owes who lunch, or who called last is far less important than maintaining the friendship with lunch and calls. Even the truest of friends can forget at times. It's really not hard for the ones who love you the most to get busy and forget to call. Cut them some slack, because if they were to be totally honest with you, they probably often cut you some slack too. Especially avoid damaging feuds and grudges. Life is too short, and your friends are too valuable for such pettiness.

5. **Do the little things.** When a long conversation isn't possible, have a short one. If you are passing through their

town with only enough time for a brief stop, take the opportunity. A brief visit is better than no visit at all. If they do something you appreciate, no matter how small, say thanks.

6. **Stay focused on the positive.** Yes, even you have weaknesses and strange quirks in the eyes of others. So forget about the things you wish were different in your friend. If you have chosen them, and they have chosen you to be a good friend, it must be that their good points far outweigh their bad ones.

7. **Be accessible.** Not only is it important to be there when your friends need you, but at certain times in your life, it can be just as important to be available for making new friends. This is particularly true in the lives of older people. I've often heard it said that one of the greatest problems confronting older people today is loneliness. The negative aspect of the aging process is that friends and family die. When faced with such loss, rather than staying home alone nurturing your sorrow, frequent places where new people can be met and new friends made.

Consider these words from the inspired pen of Solomon, the man whose name is synonymous with wisdom, found in the book of Ecclesiastes chapter 4 verses 9 through 12. *Two people are better off than one, for they can help each other succeed. 10 If one person falls, the other can reach out and help. But someone who falls alone is in real trouble. 11 Likewise, two people lying close together can keep each other warm. But how can one be warm alone? 12 A person standing alone can be attacked and defeated, but two can stand back-to-back and conquer. Three are even better, for a triple-braided cord is not easily broken.* (Holy Bible, New Living Translation).

EMPOWERED POSSIBILITIES

Shared laughter is one of the most effective tools for keeping relationships fresh and exciting. All emotional sharing builds strong and lasting relationship bonds, but sharing laughter and play adds joy, vitality, and resilience. And humor is a powerful and effective way to heal resentments, disagreements, and hurts. Laughter unites people during difficult times.

Now that I've sold you on the value of friendship and of being a good friend, let me share some bad news with you. *(I have convinced you, haven't I? If I haven't, please go back to the beginning of this chapter and read it again, a little more carefully this time.)* Recent studies suggest that Americans have significantly fewer friends today than they did twenty years ago.

It seems that, more and more, we are victimized by our own creative success. The very technology that allows us to work harder and produce more is robbing us of our friendships. Thanks to technology, for many jobs, location and proximity to coworkers are no longer essential. Working from home, while convenient and desirable from many aspects, deprives the worker from the beneficial dynamics of face-to-face contact.

In most of these arrangements, a regular visit to the office is a good requirement. Each visit strengthens relationship bonds in ways that simply cannot be achieved online or over the telephone. In my view, videoconferencing and webinars, while efficient and cost saving, lose effectiveness unless they are regularly interspersed with face-to-face meetings.

I serve on several committees for my state professional association, which seldom, if ever, meet face-to-face. I usually forget to call in, seldom remember to read the handouts, and am therefore not nearly as useful in the affairs of the committees as I would be were we to meet face-to-face from time to time. Frankly, I don't know all the people on the committees and can't therefore attach a face to many of the voices. I don't condemn the use of electronic meeting replacements. I would, however, like to suggest that a periodic, face-to-face meeting makes them much more effective and well worth the cost in time and money to travel a central location.

As we become more efficient, we have less time for our friends. Thanks to the convenience of cell phones, e-mail, texting, Skype, Facebook, and MySpace, we are allocating less and less time to personal interaction.

While it is unlikely that any form of electronic social networking can replace direct, face-to-face interaction, there can be significant health benefits connected to the use of the rapidly expanding field of social media networks such as Twitter and Facebook, to name two. Following is a brief discussion of the probable benefits of using social media.

1. **You can form new friendships.** Thanks to such social media sites as Twitter and Facebook, it's possible to establish communication with people you have never met. Many of these people, I will never see face-to-face. Yet thanks to Facebook I can learn much about them, often enough to feel a genuine connection. Not too long ago, in fact, a gentleman with my same name, who grew up in the rather sparsely populated area of central Nebraska, where I spent much of my childhood, contacted me. He inquired about my family. He even had several family members with the same or similar names to members of my family, yet as far as we could tell there was no other connection. While interesting and even a bit eerie, it has led not nor do I expect that it will lead to friendship. On the other hand, while I remember her from high school, the friend I most often hear from on Facebook was two years ahead of me, not in my social circle, and I have no recollection of ever speaking to her. I enjoy hearing from her now.

EMPOWERED POSSIBILITIES

2. **You can stay in touch with hard-to-reach family members.** Because I'm a member of the older generation, keeping up with the busy lives of teenage grand nieces and nephews would be impossible without Facebook. They will occasionally contact me, but more often, if I'm curious, I can catch up with them by going to their Facebook page. I'm in touch via e-mail with a fairly large number of cousins. Motivated in no small part by this electronic contact, I get together with many of them at least annually.

3. **You can reconnect with old friends or long-lost family members.** Thanks to e-mail, I'm now in periodic contact with Cousin Calvin, a man I haven't seen in at least fifty years. Though I haven't told him yet, I intend to visit him in the coming year. Our occasional exchange of e-mails has convinced me that I would enjoy knowing him. If it weren't for Facebook, sadly I would know very little about my sister and her life. If I want to catch up with what's going on in the life of my old friend Paul, whom I haven't spoken with in nearly twenty-five years, all I have to do is bring up his Facebook page because he accepted me as a friend. I now know that Doug, forty-one years absent from my life, is a college professor in Canada. Since Facebook limits the size of your message to less than 350 words, it is possible to exchange brief messages with literally dozens of contacts in a relatively short amount of time.

4. **You can maintain and expand your business network.** Thanks to the wonders of the iPhone, I get the latest happenings in the world of business delivered directly to my hip (*that's where I wear my iPhone holster*) several times a day. I routinely conduct many business conversations via e-mail. In this way I avoid phone tag.

EMPOWERED POSSIBILITIES

5. **You can share your opinions with the world.** If I wanted to, I could start an intense discussion on Facebook, updating it several times a day simply by expressing my opinion on any topic of my choice. Being heard can be a challenge, but Facebook makes it easy. Today Facebook is used by politicians, consultants, and just about anyone with an axe to grind or a product to sell to get their voices heard. I can even have my own blog and probably will, if I can ever figure out just what a blog is and how it works.

6. **You will find opportunities to help other people or to get help yourself.** Whether it's in an e-mail blast or a Facebook quote, and whether it's a request for information or a plea for life-sustaining support, your messages reach the world.

The use of social media is particularly valuable for people who live in isolation, whether by design or circumstance. Physical limitations often force individuals to spend most of their life shut in their own homes. Geographic isolation can allow days to go by without any human contact. These situations are custom designed for social media. But even the best social media won't let you experience that special warmth that can only come from physical contact with another living being. Hugs, when delivered across telephone lines, are just not as good.

A hug from another human is as good as it gets, but anyone who has ever had a treasured pet knows that a cuddle with your dog or cat comes in a pretty good second. It's been shown that people who live alone but have a pet are healthier and happier and live longer than people living alone without a pet.

The benefits of social wellness in addition to the ones we've already covered include:

EMPOWERED POSSIBILITIES

- Increased comfort and contentment with you as a person- after all, if others seem to like you, why shouldn't you like yourself?
- The opportunity to get comfortable with and learn from people representing different backgrounds, nationalities, races, religions, and lifestyles- practical diversity in action
- The chance to devote your time and energy to community improvement
- Better health
- New friendships
- A greater balance in your life between responsibilities and relaxation

Before you leave this chapter, take a few moments to consider the actions that you are willing to take to improve your social wellness. In the table below, you will find a list of the social wellness improving tactics I've shared with you in this chapter. Please review the list and in the space to the left of each tactic, enter the date on which you propose to implement that tactic in your pursuit of better, stronger, and longer lasting relationships.

MY SOCIAL WELLNESS IMPROVEMENT PLAN	
DATE	SOCIAL WELLNESS IMPROVEMENT TACTICS
	Make a list of valued friends and family you haven't communicated with in a while and develop strategies for contact.
	Identify social events with a high probability for making friends and make plans to get involved.
	Identify a church, club or activity you think you will enjoy and get involved.
	Find a project where your unique talents and skills could be beneficial and participate.

MY SOCIAL WELLNESS IMPROVEMENT PLAN	
DATE	SOCIAL WELLNESS IMPROVEMENT TACTICS
	Make a list of people you would like to get to know better and start inviting them to your home or out for a meal.
	Make a list of the most common excuses you have for not being involved with other people and develop written strategies to overcome them.
	Stop holding out for the perfect friend or companion and work with the ones you have. It may surprise you to discover that often the people who irritate you the most, are best friends in the making.
	If you don't already have one, get a computer; open an e-mail account and join something like Facebook.
	Start committing unexpected acts of kindness for those around you.
	Start saying yes more often.
	If others don't talk to you, start the conversation yourself.

CHAPTER 10: A BRIEF SUMMARY

For a relatively short book, we've covered a lot of territory. I kept the book small to make it easier for you to read, yet I think I've made it just long enough to give you a solid basis for living with **Empowered Independence.** In closing, I'd like to bring it all together for you in terms as brief, succinct, and clear as I can make them.

Empowered Independence is all about living your best life successfully at any age, but particularly in your advanced years. It's about maximizing your physical and intellectual wellness so that you can stay sharp and capable at any age, even a great age. In this book, one of my goals was to explode seven myths about aging that, taken individually or collectively, continue to ruin many lives. In this chapter, we'll review each of the seven myths along with the seven truths that replace them.

The First Myth: It's the natural order of things for older people to retire, step aside, and let the young people handle things.

As with many falsehoods, there is an element of truth in the myth as stated above. At some point, older people must let the young people take a leadership role. But this does not mean that an old person ceases to engage. Retirement should not simply be a life of few commitments and responsibilities. It should be a life of carefully chosen and strategically spaced commitments and responsibilities.

EMPOWERED POSSIBILITIES

With age comes experience, and with experience comes knowledge that often leads to wisdom. It is a shame of almost criminal proportions when a knowledgeable, experienced and wise mind is allowed, even in retirement, to go to sleep. Engagement at any age is crucial to your health and sense of well-being, and no less so as you age. People who remain engaged in life, even if it is in activities completely different from those based on career and earlier life choices stay healthier, happier, and mentally sharper much longer than those who choose to sit back and do little or nothing.

Let us replace this myth with the following truth.

The First Truth: With age and experience comes wisdom that should be shared. In fact, it is in the sharing of this wisdom that long-term health and mental acuity are to be found.

Bob, a Villa resident at Waterman Village, Mount Dora Florida, visits virtually every administrative office on the fifty-five acre compound at least weekly and some of them daily. Bob notices things and shares his observations. He has even done a comprehensive analysis of the cost of leaving lights on all night. Most of his points are excellent.

Frank, a legally blind, lifelong entrepreneur, at eighty-three and squarely in the middle of our recent recession, took up stock market investing. Since he no longer sees well enough to read, his faithful wife reads a regular and broad spectrum of financial publications to him every day. Based on what he hears, he invests. As with any investor, his portfolio is up one day and down the next, but overall, I'm told, he's done well. Of almost equal value however, is the fun he's having and the benefits he's reaping through this challenging use of his brainpower.

Though his current type of investing is new territory for him, the life of an entrepreneur is not. He refuses to let his mind go to sleep and his wisdom go to waste.

EMPOWERED POSSIBILITIES

The First Principle of Empowered Independence: Engage, get involved, and participate in activities that have personal meaning to you. Engaged involvement is not only good for your physical and mental health, but it is also far more satisfying in the long run than is being a spectator.

The Second Myth: The older you get, the less you are needed.

It may be true that as you get older, and particularly when and if you retire, you are not needed in the activities that formed your career. But to say that the older you get, the less you are needed is simply not true. It isn't being needed that goes away. It is that the nature of the ways in which you are needed changes.

I have two children: a thirty-four-year-old daughter, married with two children of her own; and a thirty-one-year-old son, recently married with no children as yet. When they were babies, they needed my wife Janet and me for virtually everything in their lives. We fed them, bathed them, changed them, comforted them, encouraged them, and transported them everywhere they needed and/or wanted to go. We were really needed in those days, and often we were tired.

Eventually they learned to feed themselves. They conquered walking, and before long, they bathed themselves. Finally, they mastered the potty. What a tedious need-based task that was! They no longer needed us for all the same reasons they did as babies, but they still needed us. We still transported them everywhere they needed and/or wanted to go. When they finally learned to drive, we provided access to wheels. This we were happy to do, as their driving brought us, in addition to what we later learned were well-founded fears and concerns, freedom as well. Their clothing needs escalated in quantity, variety, and cost. They needed a college education. Eventually they needed us to help pay for weddings, assistance with major purchases such as cars and houses, and help with moving. They didn't stop needing us; the mode of the need, and the methods required to fill it, changed.

Now we are grandparents and the chain of need continues. We babysit. We even pet sit. But the most important need of all, to us and I think also to our grandchildren, is that they need us as playmates. They need us to attend their soccer games and their preschool Christmas programs. We still act as transporters from time to time, and the lunch and dinner dates are great fun. My wife, always the better homework assistant with our children, is even more effective with our grandchildren.

By now, I think, you are getting the point. As parents, we were needed and are still needed, but in different ways and for different reasons. Consider this book and the reasons why I'm writing it. I built a career on progressively learning how to serve the senior population. Now that I'm a member of that population, I'm writing down what I've learned and also speaking on the topic whenever I get a chance.

One day in the not-too-distant future, I will retire from the managing of senior communities. I will not, however, stop contributing. I will write, and I will speak on the subject to anyone who will listen. In that way, I plan to continue mattering to my profession and the people it serves. I actually believe that in my retirement, I have the potential to make a much larger contribution and therefore a greater difference than what I currently do in my work.

I'm still a good parent. I'm as active in their lives as my children want me to be. In many ways I'm much happier with myself as a grandparent that I was as a parent because, oddly enough, I'm more patient. And as I transition into the untested territory of retirement, I hope to and believe I can make a significant difference in the lives of the older people who are now my peers.

EMPOWERED POSSIBILITIES

The point is this. As you grow older, you continue to be needed. If you choose to matter, you can contribute and make a significant difference in anything you choose to be involved with. It isn't that you are no longer needed; it's just that the way in which you are needed changes and can even intensify if you let it.

The Second Truth: even though it may come at a slower pace, older people have as much value to give as younger people.

The Second Principle of Empowered Independence: Matter, make a positive difference, participate, contribute, and give back. If you do, you will be needed in the purest sense of the word, and your legacy will be worthy and memorable.

I have learned that often it is just as important to be needed as it is to have your needs met. You can and should matter to your friends and family at any and every age. You're never too old to contribute and you also never have too little to give.

There is an often told story of a little boy observed one morning, standing on a beach amid hundreds of starfish stranded there by a roguish wave. As the observer watches, the young boy is systematically, and as quickly as possible, tossing starfish, one at a time, back into the water. The observer, being an experienced adult with a practical bent on life, approaches the young boy and with all of the wisdom collected throughout his many years, says, "Son, you're wasting your time. There are far too many starfish. What you're doing can't possibly matter."

Not even pausing to look up, the young boy tossed another starfish back into the waves. Quietly, turning to the adult, he said, "It mattered to that one."

We all need to live our lives with the philosophy of that young boy. We may not be able to make a difference in many lives on a grand scale. In fact, as we get older, we may not be able to reach as many people as we once could during our prime. But we can make a difference in the life of the person or persons next to us. We can and we should make that difference at any age. Who knows? That person sitting next to you, if you give them a chance, just might make a difference in your life too.

The Third Myth: Declining physical strength is a natural and unavoidable consequence of aging.

It is possible that moving slower is a natural consequence of aging. It might even be probable that if you are a big-league bodybuilder like Jack LaLanne—who at ninety-six still worked out two hours a day: an hour and a half lifting weights and a half hour of swimming—you won't as strong at your death as you were in your prime. Jack was, however, amazingly fit and strong beyond virtually any other ninety-six-year-old. Jack LaLanne spent his life becoming as strong as he could be—so strong in fact, that when he was old, growing weaker was inevitable. Most of us aren't in his league. But, for us non-body builders, growing weaker does not have to be a natural consequence of the aging process. In fact, growing stronger is every bit as realistic as growing weaker.

We established in chapter 5 that it is possible to strengthen your muscles well beyond the age of eighty. The life of Jack LaLanne serves as proof of the possibility of maintaining prodigious physical fitness to age ninety and beyond.

The single largest source of injury as we grow older is a fall. That the caricature of older people is one of unsteady walking has made it possible for comedians such as Tim Conway to make a lot of money imitating old people as they walk. The good news is, we can walk with a steady gait even as we get older. The unsteady gait so often associated with older people is the result of poor balance. Poor balance can be caused by many things, such as weakened muscles that haven't been used enough to

EMPOWERED POSSIBILITIES

keep them strong and healthy, and by simple failure to walk enough.

Balance issues can be easily addressed with several treatments from a good physical therapist. Talk to your doctor about that.

A second issue associated with injuries from falls is lack of flexibility. Muscles that don't get used often will grow stiff. Smoking, because of its penchant for stealing oxygen from the muscles, is another source of stiff muscles. Stiff muscles are more prone to injury. Just as you can strengthen your muscles by exercising at any age, so too can you increase their flexibility by first warming them up using simple exercises, then stretching them. Even the most well-toned athlete warms up and stretches. Why then, would you think you don't need to?

The third issue contributing to injury from falls is declining bone density, once again a natural outcome of the aging process. This too, natural though it may be, can be prevented. Exercise increases bone density, resulting in thicker, stronger bones better able to resist breaking in a fall.

The Third Truth: It takes work, but you can increase your strength, flexibility, and physical capacity at literally any age.

The fact is, we are never too old to benefit from a good program of strength and flexibility improvement. Several years ago I read of one seventy-year-old who became something of a national phenomenon by taking up aggressive mountain climbing. Prior to that year she had never climbed a mountain before. In fact, if I remember correctly, she didn't even routinely walk for exercise.

Two years ago I watched a race in New York City where the oldest contestant to cross the finish line was nearly ninety, and he wasn't the last one in.

EMPOWERED POSSIBILITIES

The only question for you really, is when to begin. I suggest now. Your exciting new world will not be without pain and strain, but you'll be amazed at the things you'll be able to do.

The Third Principle of Empowered Independence: Preserve your physical fitness through exercise, stretching, and regularly giving yourself time for restoration. In simple language, work out, eat right, and take your breaks and vacations. It's not only good for your body; it's good for your brain as well.

The Fourth Myth: It's best to expect the worst. That way you're always ready, and you're never surprised.

What difference does attitude make anyway? If I'm having a bad day I certainly have the right to be upset about it. Life is tough. Why sugarcoat it?

Several years ago I read a potentially life-changing book entitled *Think and Grow Rich* by a gentleman with the unusual name of Napoleon Hill. Among the many memorable things he said in that book, researched and written in the early decades of the 20th century, was this simple phrase: "We become what we think about."

In other words, if we focus on our opportunities and become a possibility thinker, good things are more likely to happen. On the other hand, if we spend our time worrying about potential problems, not only will we miss the opportunities hidden in them, but the problems themselves inevitably get worse.

Years ago I learned that the main reason most people are not able to sustain weight loss over the long run is that they never change their internal image of themselves. They may fervently want to be thin but if they obsess about all the weight they need to lose and all of the choice treats they have to give up, they are

EMPOWERED POSSIBILITIES

very likely, if not to remain fat, at least to go right back up in the weight as soon as the diet is over.

That is an example of a negative attitude in its worst expression. I want to be thin, but all I can think about is how fat I am. Therefore, even though I'm pounding my head against the wall of a difficult and challenging diet, I may not take the weight off and even if I do, I'm very likely put it back on again. I've lived this teeter-totter cycle in my own life no less than three times in the last thirty years. It really is about attitude. Even though I fervently longed for an attitude that would lead me to a lean, mean, and athletically preened physique, I have never stayed thin for longer than six months. In sad fact, I've managed to pack on at least an extra ten pounds each time, beyond my most recent starting point. My attitude, so far, has prevented much desired permanent weight loss. What else is it keeping from me? For that matter, what about you?

Two different research studies, spaced several years apart, proved that people with a positive attitude live eight to ten years longer and better than people with a negative attitude. Attitude is a major differentiator between success and failure in all things.

The Fourth Truth: focusing on the negative shortens your life, reduces your satisfaction, and makes you unpleasant to be around.

The story is told of a very wise man who liked to sit at the gate to his city. Because he was so widely known for his wisdom, people journeyed from all over the region to seek his counsel. It was very rare to find him alone. One day a stranger stopped by.

"What are the people like in this city?" asked the stranger. "I am thinking of moving here and would like to know a little bit about what I'm getting into before I make my final decision."

EMPOWERED POSSIBILITIES

The wise man paused for a few moments, studying the stranger carefully. Finally he said, "Before I answer your question, tell me what the people are like in your current city."

Without hesitation the stranger responded, "Oh, they're very unpleasant people, constantly bickering, feuding and stabbing each other in the back. It is so bad I can't stand it, and that's why I'm thinking of moving."

Somewhat sadly the wise man replied, "I really don't think you would enjoy living in this city either, for the people here are much like the ones you describe where you come from. This is not the city for you."

Thanking him profusely, the stranger returned to the road, traveling on, never even entering the city to look around.

Less than two hours later a second stranger came by. This stranger too, sought a new home and asked the wise man to tell him what kind of people lived in this city.

When asked by the wise man to describe the kind of people in the city he was coming from, the stranger replied, "They are wonderful. We all get along so well. We support and help each other. I wouldn't think of leaving if I wasn't being transferred."

Rising to his feet and with a big smile on his face, the wise man extended his hand in welcome, saying to the stranger, "I'm sure you will be happy here, for our people are just like those you know in your home city."

Expressing profuse gratitude the stranger entered the city, excitedly seeking his new home.

As I said, the opinion of this wise man was so valued that he was seldom alone. This day was no exception. In fact, many of the people gathered around him for the conversation with the second stranger had also witnessed his conversation with the first. They were puzzled.

"Why," they asked, "Did you give each stranger such radically different answers?"

"The reason is quite simple," replied the wise man. "The first stranger, because of his attitude, expects to find contrary people and does not stop looking until he identifies them. The second stranger expects to find friendly and kind people and seldom has trouble locating them. No matter where each stranger lives, they will find the kinds of people their attitudes lead them to expect."

Most of the time our attitudes create our reality or as a good friend of mine likes to say, your attitude determines your altitude. How high does your attitude let you fly?

The Fourth Principle of Empowered Independence: Optimize your opportunities with attitudes of possibility, be a possibility thinker and don't get bogged down with impossibility thinking.

The Fifth Myth: Even if there is a God, he couldn't possibly be interested in my meager, little affairs.

Even though in today's world it isn't politically correct, in many venues, to speak of God, it is a well-proven fact that faith, prayer, and meditation come with healing powers of often mythical proportions.

There is great comfort in being able to share our burdens and concerns with a higher power. While my personal understanding of God is formed by a strong Christian ethic, I've learned that regardless of who your God is, what you call Him, and how you communicate, the power is there and available to you.

EMPOWERED POSSIBILITIES

Faith becomes particularly important as we age. Stories of miraculous healings in response to prayer are too numerous to count. Faith and belief, expressed in both word and action, seem to be the key to tapping this power.

So while I recommend in this book no specific system of faith, I do urge you to practice one. The power emanating from a strong, sustaining belief in a higher power outside the self is truly awesome.

The Fifth Truth: The older we get, the more we realize how important our God is to us and how much his love and support sustains us. We only have to believe and the power is ours.

The Fifth Principle of Empowered Independence: Worship and wield the energy and strength that comes from putting your faith in a higher power.

The Sixth Myth: The older you get, the more forgetful you become, and there isn't much you can do about it.

If your memory does get poorer as you age, it's seldom solely because you're getting old. While some older people are unfortunately born with a tendency to develop dementia, most, nearly 70 percent in fact, weaken their memory primarily because they don't challenge it often enough. Just as your body's muscles deteriorate if you don't use them, so will your brain.

Clearly, mental sharpness to the end of your life is possible for most that are willing to go to the trouble of continuous learning, experimentation, and adventure. If you feel like your memory isn't what it used to be, start challenging it. Learn a new language. Take up crossword puzzles and other challenging memory games. Exercise and become more socially involved. For most of us, unless we have dementia, and only 37 percent of us who reach the age of eighty-five will, we can actually sharpen our mental acuity.

EMPOWERED POSSIBILITIES

If you feel like you're losing your memory and ability to reason, there are two possible reasons that are far more likely than age-related mental decline. The first is mental inactivity, and the second is damaging prescription drug interactions. Don't give up on your brain before you have to. If inactivity is the source of your mental fogginess, rescue your brain from the prison of inactivity most probably built by you. If you suspect drug interaction issues, a visit to your pharmacist should clear that up for you.

The Sixth Truth: A regular program of physical fitness combined with constant exploration and learning can, for most of us, keep our minds as sharp as ever they were.

The Sixth Principle of Empowered Independence: Expand your brainpower through lifelong learning. There is a joke making the rounds that goes like this. Of all the things I miss, I miss my mind the most. I hope I've convinced you that your mind doesn't have to go missing if you'll just keep using it. If you let your brain go to sleep, it can be hard to wake it up. Therefore, keep it awake. If it's already dozing, shake it, challenge it, dare it, and then enjoy its rebirth.

The Seventh Myth: The older you get, the more likely you are to end up alone and friendless.

If you allow the above myth to be true in your life, you're doing great damage to your potential for maximum good. Put simply, people with a strong social support system are much healthier than are those who have few if any friends.

As we age, it is far too easy to give in to the aches and pains that increasingly dog our days. It seems far simpler to just stay home. Ultimately it's easy to let physical disability, real, magnified, and imagined, justify turning down those invitations, which eventually decline in number and finally disappear.

EMPOWERED POSSIBILITIES

Of the seven principles I've shared with you in this book, it's close to impossible to say which is the most important. However, it wouldn't surprise me if research should show that maintaining relationships is the number one source of good health and life satisfaction.

Think about it. Friends give you a reason to come out of your pain walled, and usually self-imposed protective cocoon. It's easier to exercise if you have friends. You're more likely to eat a proper diet if you're not eating alone. It is more fun to be engaged in meaningful activity when you're working with friends. With a close circle of friends, it's impossible not to know that you matter to someone and are needed. Activities with friends give you something to look forward to and in the process, improve your attitude.

Often, seeing our friends is the main impetus for attending worship services where, in the process, we tap into a tremendous power. Conversations with friends expand our mental acuity. Good relationships are the glue that holds all of the concepts of Empowered Independence together.

So if you find yourself tempted to allow your aches and pains to guide you into a life of solitary isolation, conquer those aches and pains. Get out and socialize. It will lengthen and enrich your life. Furthermore, you will notice one day, to your pleasant surprise that your body suffers from far fewer aches and pains.

The Seventh Truth: Relationships do change with age. Old friends die. People who age successfully simply make new friends. It is unlikely that very many of us have the luxury of being so desirable that people are knocking on our doors anxious to become our friends. But there are people out there looking for friendship too. If we just go where they're likely to be, we'll find them.

EMPOWERED POSSIBILITIES

The Seventh Principle of Empowered Independence: Relationships and a broad range of networks are essential to life success and whole person wellness at any and every age.

So here we are nearing the end of this book. I have enjoyed writing it and I hope you enjoyed reading. In writing it, I have learned much. In reading it I hope you will learn much too. My personal mission, shared with my company Waterman Communities, Inc., is to create environments where people of all ages can age successfully and live their personal best life. This book presents the roadmap for how to do it. Whether you follow the paths outlined in this book is completely up to you. Thanks for doing me the honor of reading it.

The book began with a promise; it must, therefore, close with a challenge. You will find that challenge in the next and final brief chapter.

EPILOGUE: THE CHALLENGE

Well, you made it. You finished my book. I am proud, pleased, and gratified.

I began on the first page with a bold, some might even say audacious, promise. I then proceeded to develop and share strategies designed to help you capture the benefits of my promise. I'd like now to conclude with a challenge. Here it is.

EMPOWER your own personal brand of independence. You can do it. I know you can. I also know it will likely not be easy.

We didn't make it in 1967

Thanks to my Uncle Albert, I grew up with a love of travel and a strong need to see and be in mountains not less than once per year. Albert's passion was Colorado. He knew nearly every mountain by altitude, location, and, it seemed, as a personal friend. In 1967 we, along with my parents and my sister, made what was

EMPOWERED POSSIBILITIES

my first assault on Pike's Peak. We didn't reach the top—not even close. Our trusty 1959 Ford overheated two-thirds of the way up and we had to turn around. It would be more than thirty years before my next try, which also would fail—this time due to a late spring snow blocking both the road and the cog rail tracks.

Pike's Peak is a serious mountain, but as mountains go, at just over 14,100 feet it is far from the tallest. It is, in fact, roughly half the height of Mount Everest. Yet Pike's Peak is a phenomenon in its own way. First, you can drive your car to the top as we tried to do in 1966. Few roads in the world, much less the United States, claim that altitude.

By far the most unique aspect of Pike's Peak, however, is its geographic placement. Perched on the eastern edge of the Rocky Mountains, it towers above its surroundings. It first appears on the horizon from more than one hundred miles away. You can clearly identify it from the city of Denver if you are lucky enough to be there on a smog-free day.

On a cold, misty day in late September of 1999, my son Jeff and I, in our rented Cadillac approached the peak for my third attempt. My soon to be twenty-year-old son was driving. I drank in the view from the shotgun seat. It really is great when the kids get old enough to drive!

At just over 14,000 feet, Pike's Peak is nearly three miles high in vertical measure. The road to the top, however, stretches nineteen miles from the entrance gate to the summit. The initial assent is easy and pleasant. The incline is gentle and the road is surrounded on both sides with grassy meadows and panoramic mountain vistas. It was a great day and Jeff—who loves travel as much as I do—and I were relaxed and excited. Beautiful scenery, comfortable father/son companionship, a broad and well paved road, and a brand new Cadillac for Pete's sake; what could be better?!!

EMPOWERED POSSIBILITIES

As we drove higher, the road got narrower but we barely noticed. We could see for dozens of miles and even in the mist, the scenery was breathtaking. The powerful engine in our Cadillac devoured the miles with little effort. This mountain was ours!!

At ten thousand feet, things began to change. The trees disappeared; not much of a problem, but so did the pavement, and a little further up the road, so also did the rest of the mountains. The only thing left to us was the car, the gravel road with no guardrails, and emptiness in the misty sky. We had, by now, climbed so much higher than the surrounding mountains that we could no longer see them unless we looked way over the barrier free side of the road. We didn't want to do that. Staring straight ahead, all we saw were the next switchback and the road devoured by the thickening mist. Thus began the first stirrings of acrophobia, the fear of heights.

Now, tensed in my seat and studiously avoiding glances into the emptiness to the side of the car, I took no small pleasure in the fact that my stalwart 6 foot 5 inch nineteen year old son was driving and I wasn't. Suddenly and without warning, Jeff slammed on the brakes, right there close to the middle of the narrowing gravel road and about halfway between two switchbacks.

Slamming the steering wheel with his doubled fists, he said, "Dad, I can't do this anymore. You'll have to drive."

Apparently acrophobia is genetic in its origins. Who knew?

The last thing I wanted to do just then was to drive forward to the next switchback, where for all that I could see the road simply dropped off the mountainside into oblivion. Well, it was almost the last thing. The very last thing I wanted to do was remain there in that increasingly hellish limbo.

EMPOWERED POSSIBILITIES

With a knotting unpleasant churning in my stomach and the bile of real, palpable fear rising in my throat, I took the wheel. We were 3,000 feet from the summit. Backing up simply wasn't an option. We had come too far and I had wanted for too long to get to the top. Anyway, if I wasn't going to look over the side, I certainly wasn't going to look backwards. Besides, if falling off seemed likely by driving on, how could backing up be any better? And we certainly weren't going to do a three point turnaround on that high and rocky, barrier-free road, so forward we went.

I had not known that 3,000 feet could be so far, take so long, and offer so much challenge. As each switchback approached, I just knew we were going to drop off the mountain. But we didn't. We made it to the top and just like that, fears were forgotten in the exhilaration of accomplishment and the incredible view that even in the mist, at that altitude, and in a light swirl of snow, went on for well over one hundred miles.

The point is this. It was a mountain and it scared us. We wanted to be at the top, but what we had to go through to get there was downright scary even if our fears were totally without basis. We wouldn't drop off the mountain, but that didn't keep us from fearing that we would.

Life and the challenges it brings can be fearsome. It took me thirty years and two failed attempts to reach the top of my mountain, but when I got there, the view was worth it and the fear, soon forgotten. I've been up again

EMPOWERED POSSIBILITIES

since, that time by cog railroad, but I hope to attempt the drive again this fall.

My challenge to you is this. Your path to living your personal best life may be mountainous and fearsome. Walk it anyway. The view from the top is well worth the effort.

www.ingramcontent.com/pod-product-compliance
Lightning Source LLC
Chambersburg PA
CBHW060521100426

42743CB00009B/1401